Business Analysis ®
Competency Model

v4

COMPREHENSIVE EDITION®

IIBA® International Institute of Business Analysis™

International Institute of Business Analysis, Toronto, Ontario, Canada.

Version 1.0 published 2008. Version 2.0 published 2010. Version 3.0 published 2011. Version 4.0 published 2017.

ISBN-13: 978-1-927584-06-4

Any inquiries regarding this publication, requests for usage rights for the material included herein, or corrections should be sent by email to bok@iiba.org.

Table of Contents

Preface

IIBA® was founded in Toronto, Canada in October of 2003 to support the business analysis community by:

- creating and developing awareness and recognition of the value and contribution of the business analyst,
- defining the *Business Analysis Body of Knowledge*® (*BABOK*®),
- providing a forum for knowledge sharing and contribution to the business analysis profession, and
- publicly recognizing and certifying qualified practitioners through an internationally acknowledged certification program.

This document is provided to the business analysis community for educational reference and research. IIBA® does not warrant that it is suitable for any other purpose and makes no expressed or implied warranty of any kind and assumes no responsibility for errors or omissions. No liability is assumed for incidental or consequential damages in connection with or arising out of the use of the information contained herein.

The goal of this revision (version 4) was to:

- modernize the Business Analysis (BA) Competency Model based on industry best practices for development of Competencies,
- streamline the assessment points,
- integrate behavioral indicators to include skill level, business analysis expertise e.g. tasks and techniques and underlying competencies,
- align it to BABOK® Guide v3.0 – the standard for Business Analysis,
- align it to the new 4-Level Certification Framework, to deliver a path for BA practitioner growth, focus on its practical application to the BA Practitioner, and
- position it as the leading resource for competency development among BA practitioners.

The major changes in this release include:

- a new five-point scale and descriptions to indicate proficiency levels for assessment,
- a decrease of assessment points (performance competencies) from over three hundred to thirty, and
- the embedding of common techniques and underlying competencies within each of the thirty performance competencies.

Introduction

1.1   About this guide

The Business Analysis Competency Model® version 4 identifies the behaviours and techniques associated with each level of business analysis, to assist readers in understanding the levels of competency in the business analysis profession.

This guide supports the four levels of IIBA's Multi-level Competency-Based Certification program by highlighting the key competency components associated with each business analysis task. This will allow professionals to identify areas of focus to promote professional development in business analysis.

1.2   What is a Competency Model?

A competency model is a framework for defining knowledge, skills, abilities, techniques, and personal characteristics that together define successful performance in a work setting, in any chosen profession.

Competency models are the foundation for important human resource functions such as recruitment and hiring, training and development, and performance management.

Competency models are also developed for specific jobs, job groups, organizations, occupations, or industries to help evaluate and grow careers.

To be effective, a competency model must both define the characteristics necessary for success and indicators that can be used to assess if individuals display that competency on the job.

Figure 1.2.1: Figure 1: Competency Model Wheel

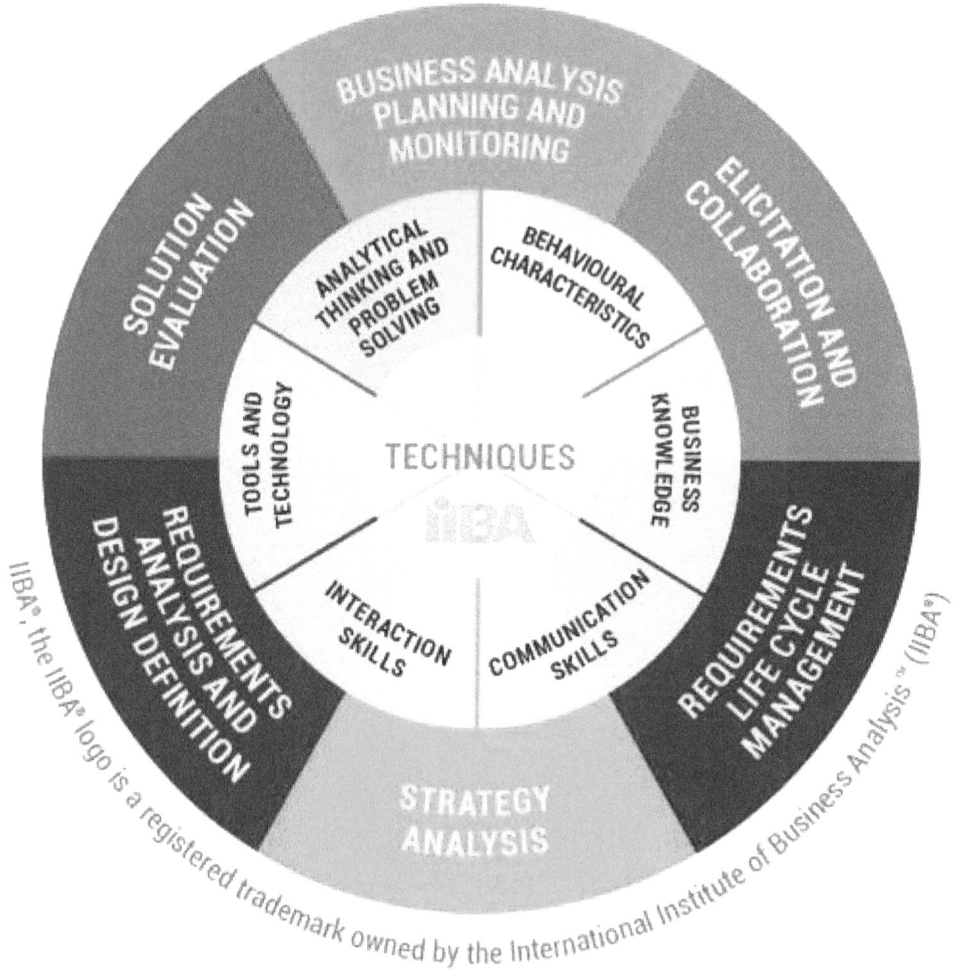

1.3   Understanding the Model

Key Concepts

Competency is the successful application of knowledge, skills, abilities, and proficiency descriptors that are expected from individuals as they progress their careers.

Experience in these areas grows as the knowledge and techniques are applied in a variety of contexts and situations.

Knowledge Areas

Knowledge Areas (KAs) from the BABOK® Guide version 3.0 (Chapters 3 - 8).

Performance Competencies

Thirty performance competencies are the base of this model, categorized by BABOK® Guide Knowledge Areas.

Underlying Competencies

Underlying Competencies, the skills, knowledge and personal characteristics that support the effective performance of business analysis, are defined in Chapter 9 of the BABOK® Guide.

Tasks

A Task is an essential piece of business analysis work that must be performed as part of business analysis. Each Task should be performed at least once during the vast majority of business analysis initiatives. Tasks are defined within each Knowledge Area of the BABOK® Guide.

Techniques

Techniques are different ways that a Task may be performed. Techniques are defined in Chapter 10 of the BABOK® Guide.

Proficiency Descriptors

The Proficiency Descriptors of the Business Analysis Competency Model are derived from the Knowledge Areas and Underlying Competencies as listed in the BABOK® Guide v3.

These describe the behaviours the business analysis professional demonstrates, drawing on his or her knowledge, skills and experience in the competency.

1.4   Who should use the Competency Model?

The Business Analysis Competency Model is a research and reference guide designed to equip BA professionals with the information needed to continuously develop skills in real-time, in order to meet the needs of organizations.

This model can be used by anyone involved directly or indirectly in the Business Analysis (BA) profession, regardless of their official job role or title. The usage and value for differing roles can be generally summarized as follows:

- Business Analysis Professionals
- Business Analysis Manager/Team Leads
- Human Resources Professionals

Business Analysis Professionals

Business Analysis Professionals can use this guide to:

- apply the six knowledge areas (KAs) from *A Guide to the Business Analysis Body of Knowledge® (BABOK® Guide) v3.* (chapters 3-8), in the context of BA roles and responsibilities performed at all levels of the profession,

- understand and assess business analysis skill levels against the thirty performance competencies and the different techniques used to demonstrate them,

- recognize the necessary behavioral indicators that are tied to the development and demonstration of underlying competencies from the BABOK® Guide (chapter 9), to further career development.

The Competency Model helps BA Professionals to:

- identify the skills, knowledge and behavioral characteristics demonstrated at all levels of the BA Profession, and

- track where they are in their career and provide the information necessary to grow in the profession.

Business Analysis Manager/Team Leads

Business Analysis Managers and Team Leads can use this guide to:

- understand the different levels of BA performance within their team,

- identify and assess a skills gap amongst individual BA team members against the performance competencies, techniques, and key behavioral indicators needed to perform successful on the job, and

- facilitate career planning discussions with individual BA team members to assist them with further career development.

The Competency Model helps Business Analysis Managers and Team leads to:

- understand what to expect when hiring a General Awareness, Practical Knowledge, Skilled, Expert or Strategist Level BA, and

- identify the skills and knowledge gaps of the BA Professional at these levels, to facilitate ongoing performance management, mentoring, coaching and career planning discussions.

Human Resource Professionals

Human Resources Professionals can use this guide to:

- research role gaps and perform deeper assessments to align roles per industry trends and benchmarks, and

- assist in the recruitment efforts to hire the right skilled level BA Professionals.

The Competency Model helps Human Resource Professionals to:

- assess training gaps with BA Management,
- hire the right BA Professionals,
- understand the value the BA Professional offers, and
- elevate the BA Professional as a leader within the organization.

1.5   How to use the competency model

Users of the Competency Model may consider the following guidance to determine the best utilization:

1. Review the BABOK® Guide Knowledge Area tasks, as listed in this guide.
2. In each task's Proficiency Descriptors section, self-assess yourself against the 5-pt scale (General Awareness to Strategist).
3. Review the next level of Proficiency Descriptors to assess what traits you will need to demonstrate to move to the level.
4. Consider the Common Techniques for each Knowledge Area task to understand how to apply them in performance of the tasks.

1.6   Copyright, Licensing, and Contact Information

Copyright Information

International Institute of Business Analysis™ (IIBA®), Toronto, Ontario, Canada.

©2017 International Institute of Business Analysis™ (IIBA®). All rights reserved.

This Business Analysis Competency Model® is not for distribution, digital transmission, resale, or reproduction in whole or part.

This document is provided to the business analysis community for educational purposes. IIBA® does not warrant that it is suitable for any other purpose and makes no expressed or implied warranty of any kind and assumes no responsibility for errors or omissions. No liability is assumed for incidental or consequential damages in connection with or arising out of the use of the information contained herein.

IIBA®, the IIBA® logo, BABOK® Guide, Business Analysis Body of Knowledge®, and Business Analysis Competency Model® are registered trademarks owned by International Institute of Business Analysis. CBAP® and CCBA® are registered trademarks owned by International Institute of Business Analysis™. Certified Business Analysis Professional, ECBA™, EEP and the EEP logo are trademarks owned by International Institute of Business Analysis.

No challenge to the status or ownership of these or any other trademarked terms contained herein is intended by the International Institute of Business Analysis.

Any inquiries regarding this publication should be sent by email to info@iiba.org.

Licensing and Permissions

IIBA Member and Purchased Copy Permissions

A member copy of the Business Analysis Competency Model® allows an IIBA member in good standing a personal use license, which grants permission to use the *Competency Model* for personal career and competency development purposes only. Members are not allowed to copy, reproduce (in part or whole) or share with others without explicit and written permission from the IIBA. Permission is granted to reproduce this document for your own personal, professional or educational use only. IIBA members and individuals may not transfer ownership of their complimentary copy. IIBA owns the copyrights to this material and international copyright law applied to this publication.

Corporate Usage Permissions

Using the Business Analysis Competency Model® in a corporate or organizational setting requires a license from IIBA®.

Organizations may purchase a corporate license to the Business Analysis Competency Model® for enterprise wide usage internal to their team or organization. The corporate license enables organizations and teams of Business Analysis Practitioners to share the Business Analysis Competency Model® and use it within the team and corporate setting. The corporate license allows organizations to post the model internally, and tailor or modify the model to their organization in accordance with the terms and conditions of the license agreement. Corporate members of IIBA® are also eligible for a discount on the corporate license.

Contact Information

For more information on licensing the Business Analysis Competency Model® in a corporate or team setting, please refer to the license agreement signed and agreed upon by your organization and the IIBA.

For any questions about the content of the Business Analysis Competency Model®, please contact info@iiba.org.

2 Proficiency Levels Legend

The following table lists the five levels of proficiency, and provides descriptors for each.

Table 2.0.1: Proficiency Levels Legend

Rating	Label	Description
5	Strategist	Someone who: • challenges the status quo to develop innovative solutions that help advance business analysis as a discipline, practice or profession, and • helps expand business analysis concepts and practices.
4	Expert	The Expert level describes someone who: • addresses any challenge or opportunity, regardless of level of complexity, • finds a way to deliver business value for any change challenge, • guides and mentors others in order to help them deliver better business outcomes, • is sought after for expertise and guidance in addressing business challenges, and • provides insight to situations that fall within (or outside of) the sphere of influence.

Table 2.0.1: Proficiency Levels Legend (Continued)

Rating	Label	Description
3	Skilled	The Skilled level describes someone who: • successfully completes straight-forward tasks and smaller, well-scoped challenges independently, and • identifies appropriate actions and modifies guidelines that have been provided to address a challenge.
2	Practical Knowledge	The Practical Knowledge level describes someone who: • needs and follows rules and guidelines to perform tasks, • adheres to prescribed ways to work in order to execute activities related to the competency, and • recognizes the key elements of the competency and why they are important.
1	General Awareness	The General Awareness level describes someone who: • has a fundamental awareness and understanding of basic skills and knowledge involved in the competency.

3 Business Analysis Planning and Monitoring

3.1 Plan Business Analysis Approach

Definition

The purpose of Plan Business Analysis Approach is to define an appropriate method to conduct business analysis activities.

Proficiency Descriptors

For descriptions on what each of the five levels mean, refer to the Proficiency Levels Legend.

5 - Strategist

- Develop and proactively drive adoption of tools, templates, and processes for planning a business analysis approach.

- Document rules and best practices for selecting a communication method.

- Create new and innovative formal and informal processes, tools, or techniques that others can leverage during discovery to isolate critical information.

- Develop and drive adoption of new methodologies as appropriate.

- Apply foresight when connecting concepts to enterprise components.

- Develop an innovative approach for using new tools, templates and processes that:

  - explain the rationale for adoption, and

  - invite intentional feedback and opinions from others.

- Develop a network of Subject Matter Experts (SMEs) inside and outside of the organization using methods such as:

  - contributing knowledge/skill into the network, and

  - drawing knowledge/skill from the network appropriately.

- Create innovative ways of performing this task using common techniques.

- Demonstrate Expert Proficiency Descriptors.

4 - Expert

- Consistently plan a business analysis approach for complex situations.

- Consistently uncover emotional drivers of stakeholders and develop business analysis approach messaging accordingly.

- Play multiple roles within activities prescribed by a methodology.

- Apply insight and business acumen when connecting concepts as they relate to different aspects of the enterprise.

- Ask relevant questions to uncover and understand organizational needs to ensure that the planning activity covers enterprise breadth and depth.

- Have been frequently engaged by peers for advice and support.

- Guide others on planning business analysis approach and required activities.

- Coach others on applying active listening and discovery skills.

- Guide others on how to effectively use common techniques.

- Demonstrate Skilled Proficiency Descriptors.

3 - Skilled

- Tailor the business approach based on the audience's known preferences/ needs by:

  - adapting the preferred verbal & non-verbal communication style to the needs of the situation and the individual, and

  - using active listening and discovery skills to understand "real" issues/ needs and build rapport.

- Select the appropriate business analysis approach, and obtain feedback and agreement on the selection from others.

- Determine the appropriate level of formality that is required for the business analysis approach.

- Identify the required business analysis activities.

- Consider the timing of business analysis work within the context of the overall change.

- Assess the complexity and size of the change and the overall risk factors for the change.

- Demonstrate capability in multiple analysis methodologies.

- Demonstrate an understanding of the organization's nuances and how to get things done.

- Analyze and use a holistic view of people, processes and technology to understand the enterprise.

- Execute common techniques independently.

2 - Practical Knowledge

- Plan a business analysis approach for complex situations with support from others.

- Plan a business analysis approach by following examples from others for less complex situations.

- Have a basic knowledge of, and can follow, instructions for common techniques.

1 - General Awareness

- Understand the importance of planning stakeholder engagement.

- Have an awareness of common techniques.

Common Techniques

Table 3.1.1: Plan Business Analysis Approach- Common Techniques

Common Techniques	Usage
Brainstorming	Used to identify possible business analysis activities, techniques, risks and other relevant items to help build the business analysis approach.
Business Cases*	Used to understand whether elements of the problem or opportunity are especially time-sensitive, high-value, or whether there is any particular uncertainty around elements of the possible need or solution.
Document Analysis	Used to review existing organizational assets that might assist in planning the approach.
Estimation	Used to determine how long it may take to perform business analysis activities.
Financial Analysis*	Used to assess how different approaches (and the supported delivery options) affect the value delivered.
Functional Decomposition	Used to break down complex business analysis processes or approaches into more feasible components.
Interviews	Used to help build the plan with an individual or small group.
Item Tracking	Used to track any issues raised during planning activities with stakeholders. Can also track risk related items raised during discussions when building the approach.
Lessons Learned	Used to identify an enterprise's previous experience (both successes and challenges) with planning business analysis approach.
Process Modelling	Used to define and document the business analysis approach.
Reviews*	Used to validate the selected business analysis approach with stakeholders.
Risk Analysis and Management*	Used to assess risks in order to select the proper business analysis approach.

Table 3.1.1: Plan Business Analysis Approach- Common Techniques

Common Techniques	Usage
Survey or Questionnaire	Used to identify possible business analysis activities, techniques, risks and other relevant items to help build the business analysis approach.
Workshops	Used to help build the plan in a team setting.

3.2   Plan Stakeholder Engagement

Definition

The purpose of Plan Stakeholder Engagement is to plan an approach to maintain effective working relationships with key stakeholders.

Proficiency Descriptors

For descriptions on what each of the five levels mean, refer to the Proficiency Levels Legend.

5 - Strategist

- Develop engagement strategies to support organizational transformation.

- Develop stakeholder engagement strategies to address stakeholders that resist change.

- Engage others in a discussion where they share information with me that they are not willing to share with other individuals.

- Capture best practices in planning stakeholder engagement and broadcast them to the business analysis community.

- Create innovative ways of performing this task using common techniques.

- Demonstrate Expert Proficiency Descriptors.

4 - Expert

- Lead others with complex stakeholder engagement.

- Effectively manage difficult personalities on a team and resolve issues if they arise.

- Have been engaged by stakeholders with their open feedback and opinions.

- Proactively develop a meeting frequency to assess progress (e.g. weekly, bi-weekly), and

    - find a balance between "over-meeting" and "under-meeting" with relevant stakeholders.

- Clearly communicate concepts to relevant stakeholders, and

  - follow up to verify stakeholder understanding and approval.

- Develop a network of SMEs within the organization.

- Coach others on applying active listening and discovery skills.

- Guide others on how to effectively use common techniques.

- Demonstrate Skilled Proficiency Descriptors.

3 - Skilled

- Perform stakeholder analysis.

- Define the level of stakeholder collaboration that will be required to support the change.

- Identify appropriate stakeholder communication needs to support the change.

- Ensure key stakeholders understand and agree to the business analysis approach.

- Facilitate stakeholder meetings.

- Demonstrate an understanding of the organization's nuances and how to get things done.

- Analyze and use a holistic view of people, processes and technology to understand the enterprise.

- Use active listening and discovery skills to understand "real" issues/needs and build rapport.

- Use common techniques.

2 - Practical Knowledge

- Plan stakeholder meetings when an issue arises and on an as-needed basis.

- Obtain stakeholder feedback and consensus on issues and resolutions as they arise.

- Have a basic knowledge of, and can follow, instructions for common techniques.

1 - General Awareness

- Understand the importance of planning stakeholder engagement.

- Have an awareness of common techniques.

Common Techniques

Table 3.2.1: Plan Stakeholder Engagement - Common Techniques

Common Techniques	Usage
Brainstorming	Used to produce the stakeholder list and identify stakeholder roles and responsibilities.
Business Rules Analysis	Used to identify stakeholders who were the source of the business rules.
Document Analysis	Used to review existing organizational assets that might assist in planning stakeholder engagement.
Interviews	Used to interact with specific stakeholders to gain more information or knowledge about stakeholder groups
Lessons Learned	Used to identify an enterprise's previous experience (both successes and challenges) with planning stakeholder engagement
Mind Mapping*	Used to identify potential stakeholders and help understand the relationships between them.
Organizational Modelling	Used to determine if the organizational units or people listed have any unique needs and interests that should be considered. Organizational models describe the roles and functions in the organization and the ways in which stakeholders interact which can help to identify stakeholders who will be affected by a change.
Process Modelling	Used to categorize stakeholders by the systems that support their business processes.
Risk Analysis & Management*	Used to identify risks to the initiative resulting from stakeholder attitudes or the inability of key stakeholders to participate in the initiative.
Scope Modelling	Used to develop scope models to show stakeholders that fall outside the scope of the solution but still interact with it in some way.

Table 3.2.1: Plan Stakeholder Engagement - Common Techniques

Common Techniques	Usage
Stakeholder Lists, Maps, or Personas	Used to depict the relationship of stakeholders to the solution and to one another.
Survey or Questionnaire	Used to identify shared characteristics of a stakeholder group.
Workshops	Used to interact with groups of stakeholders to gain more information about stakeholder groups.

3.3   Plan Business Analysis Governance

Definition

The purpose of Plan Business Analysis Governance is to develop effective decision making and approval processes to manage requirements and designs.

Proficiency Descriptors

For descriptions on what each of the five levels mean, refer to the Proficiency Levels Legend.

5 - Strategist

- Develop and proactively drive adoption of tools, templates, and processes to help others produce effective decision making and approval processes.

- Develop an innovative approach for using new tools, templates, and processes that:
  - explain the rationale for adoption, and
  - invite intentional feedback and opinions from others.

- Develop a network of Subject Matter Experts (SMEs) inside and outside of the organization and do the following:
  - contribute knowledge/skill into the network, and
  - draw knowledge/skill from the network appropriately.

- Create new methods for locating data and how to analyze its accuracy and importance.

- Capture best practices for business analysis governance and broadcast them to the business analysis community.

- Create innovative ways of performing this task using common techniques.

- Demonstrate Expert Proficiency Descriptors.

4 - Expert

- Lead others with developing effective business analysis governance.

- Collaborate with others to obtain feedback and opinions about business analysis governance tactics.

- Consistently develop effective change control processes for complex requirements and designs.

- Have been recognized, internally, as someone who can facilitate decision making and develop processes.

- Have been recognized as an authority in several analysis methodologies and have been:

  - asked by leadership to spearhead change in methodologies, and

  - asked by peers for advice and support.

- Coach others on how to assess situations in order to make the most informed decisions about which course of action to pursue.

- Guide others on how to effectively use common techniques.

- Demonstrate Skilled Proficiency Descriptors.

3 - Skilled

- Identify an effective decision making process.

- Invite feedback and opinions from others on the process.

- Develop an effective change control process for requirements and designs.

- Plan an effective prioritization process for requirements and designs.

- Plan an effective approval process for the deliverables that will be produced.

- Demonstrate capability in multiple analysis methodologies.

- Demonstrate an understanding of the organization's nuances and how to get things done.

- Make and help others make the best decision based on appropriate criteria, such as:

  - business need,

  - opportunities,

  - risk,

  - compliance, and

  - the ability to achieve the desired outcome.

- Use common techniques.

2 - Practical Knowledge

- Can plan an approval process based on what has been developed by others.

- Have a basic knowledge of, and can follow, instructions for common techniques.

1 - General Awareness

- Understand the importance of having an effective approval process to manage requirements and designs.

- Have an awareness of the common techniques.

Common Techniques

Table 3.3.1: Plan Business Analysis Governance - Common Techniques

Common Techniques	Usage
Brainstorming	Used to generate an initial list of potential stakeholder names who may need approval roles in the defined governance process.
Document Analysis	Used to evaluate existing governance processes or templates.
Interviews	Used to identify possible decision-making, change control, approval, or prioritization approaches and participants with an individual or small group.
Item Tracking	Used to track any issues that arise when planning a governance approach.
Lessons Learned	Used to find if past initiatives have identified valuable experiences with governance that can be leveraged on current or future initiatives.
Organizational Modelling	Used to understand roles/responsibilities within the organization in an effort to define a governance approach that involves the right stakeholders.
Process Modelling	Used to document the process or method for governing business analysis.
Reviews*	Used to review the proposed governance plan with key stakeholders.

Table 3.3.1: Plan Business Analysis Governance - Common Techniques

Common Techniques	Usage
Survey or Questionnaire	Used to identify possible decision-making, change control, approval, or prioritization approaches and participants.
Workshops	Used to identify possible decision-making, change control, approval, or prioritization approaches and participants within a team setting.

* Typically used by those from Skilled through Strategist. Others may use them with varying degrees of adeptness, independence or understanding, as illustrated by the performance expectations for each of the subsequent lower levels.

3.4   Plan Business Analysis Information Management

Definition

The purpose of Plan Business Analysis Information Management is to develop an effective approach for managing business analysis information.

Proficiency Descriptors

For descriptions on what each of the five levels mean, refer to the Proficiency Levels Legend.

5 - Strategist

- Develop a new organizational structure for managing business analysis information.

- Monitor the market for technologies/processes to manage business analysis information.

- Develop and drive adoption of new methodologies as appropriate, and:

    - develop tools, templates, and processes to support those methodologies.

- Apply foresight when connecting concepts to enterprise components.

- Develop training materials and "tips" that stakeholders can leverage to improve their efficiency in using business analysis tools.

- Develop an innovative approach for using new tools, templates and processes that:
    - explain the rationale for adoption, and
    - invite intentional feedback and opinions from others.
- Develop a network of Subject Matter Experts (SMEs) inside and outside of the organization using methods such as:
    - contributing knowledge/skill into the network.
    - drawing knowledge/skill from the network appropriately.
- Create innovative ways of performing this task using common techniques.
- Demonstrate Expert Proficiency Descriptors.

4 - Expert

- Lead others in developing effective approaches for managing business analysis information.
- Collaborate with others to obtain feedback and opinions on the selected approaches.
- Determine the appropriate level of abstraction for business analysis information in complex environments.
- Consistently synthesize complex data from disparate sources and understand how they impact the enterprise or organization.
- Recognized internally as an authority in locating even hard-to-find information, and
    - have been frequently engaged by peers for support.
- Consistently identify and leverage the appropriate business analysis tools based on the information and purpose of the task.
- Coach others on how to effectively use business analysis tools.
- Guide others on how to effectively use common techniques.
- Demonstrate Skilled Proficiency Descriptors.

3 - Skilled

- Determine how business analysis information will be organized.
- Obtain agreement from others on how business analysis information will be organized.
- Determine the appropriate level of abstraction for business analysis information for each stakeholder.
- Plan the traceability approach.
- Plan for requirements reuse.
- Determine how business analysis information will be stored and accessed.

- Identify what attributes will be used for ongoing management of requirements and designs.

- Demonstrate capability in multiple analysis methodologies.

- Use appropriate business analysis tools for managing business analysis information.

- Demonstrate an understanding of the organization's nuances and how to get things done.

- Analyze and use a holistic view of people, processes and technology to understand the enterprise.

- Use common techniques.

2 - Practical Knowledge

- Can plan traceability and requirements reuse approaches based on what has been developed by others.

- Can follow pre-determined instructions for storing/accessing information.

- Have a basic knowledge of, and can follow, instructions for common techniques.

1 - General Awareness

- Understand the importance of managing business analysis information.

- Have an awareness of the need to develop a way in which people can efficiently access and use business analysis information.

- Have an awareness of common techniques.

Common Techniques

Table 3.4.1: Plan Business Analysis Information Management- Common Techniques

Common Techniques	Usage
Brainstorming	Used to help stakeholders uncover their business analysis information management needs.
Interviews	Used to help specific stakeholders uncover their business analysis information management needs.
Item Tracking	Used to track issues with current information management processes.
Lessons Learned	Used to create a source of information for analyzing approaches for efficiently managing business analysis information.

Table 3.4.1: Plan Business Analysis Information Management- Common Techniques (Continued)

Common Techniques	Usage
Mind Mapping*	Used to identify and categorize the kinds of information that need to be managed.
Process Modelling	Used to document the process or method for managing business analysis information.
Survey or Questionnaire	Used to ask stakeholders to provide input into defining business analysis information management.
Workshops	Used to uncover business analysis information management needs in a group setting.

3.5　Identify Business Analysis Performance Improvements

Definition

The purpose of Identify Business Analysis Performance improvements is to assess business analysis work and plan improvement, where required.

Proficiency Descriptors

For descriptions on what each of the five levels mean, refer to the Proficiency Levels Legend.

5 - Strategist

- Develop new processes to identify and overcome business performance issues.

- Develop nontraditional ideas for identifying business analysis performance improvement opportunities.

- Create new tools and strategies for identifying innovative solutions.

- Develop an innovative approach for using new tools, templates and processes that:

  - explain the rationale for adoption, and

  - invite intentional feedback and opinions from others.

- Continually monitor processes, seeking opportunities for improvement.

- Recognized by leadership as an authority in analyzing performance and developing improvement plans, and

    - have been frequently assigned to oversee high-visibility and/or challenging initiatives.

- Create innovative ways of performing this task using common techniques.

- Demonstrate Expert Proficiency Descriptors.

4 - Expert

- Lead others to identify and correct improvement opportunities with business analysis performance.

- Collaborate with others to obtain feedback and opinions to correct improvement opportunities with business analysis performance.

- Consistently identify and correct issues with business analysis work, and independently plan improvement efforts—even for complex issues.

- Receptive to nontraditional ways of learning ideas.

- Use a structured approach for creative solutions to complex problems.

- Evaluate what worked, what did not, and what could be done differently next time.

- Recognized by colleagues as an authority in analyzing performance and developing improvement plans, and

    - have been frequently engaged by peers for support.

- Guide others on how to effectively use common techniques.

- Demonstrate Skilled Proficiency Descriptors

3 - Skilled

- Report on business analysis performance.

- Identify business analysis performance measures that can be used.

- Assess business analysis performance measures.

- Recommend actions for improving business analysis performance.

- Demonstrate an ability to learn quickly and willingly.

- Adapt to and embrace changing situations as an opportunity, rather than an obstacle.

- Think creatively and help others to think creatively to identify innovative solutions.

- Use common techniques.

2 - Practical Knowledge

- Independently identify and develop performance improvement plans for simple challenges, with guidance.

- Execute the improvement plans developed by others.

- Have a basic knowledge of, and can follow, instructions for common techniques.

1 - General Awareness

- Understand the importance of continually monitoring, assessing, and improving business analysis performance.

- Have an awareness of common techniques.

Common Techniques

Table 3.5.1: Identify Business Analysis Performance Improvements - Common Techniques

Common Techniques	Usage
Brainstorming	Used to generate ideas for improvement opportunities.
Interviews	Used to gather assessments of business analysis performance.
Item Tracking	Used to track issues that occur during the performance of business analysis for later resolution.
Lessons Learned	Used to identify recommended changes to business analysis processes, deliverables, templates, and other organizational process assets that can be incorporated into the current initiative and future work.
Metrics and Key Performance Indicators (KPIs)	Used to determine what metrics are appropriate for assessing business analysis performance and how they may be tracked.
Observation	Used to witness business analysis performance.
Process Analysis	Used to analyze existing business analysis processes and identify opportunities for improvement.

Table 3.5.1: Identify Business Analysis Performance Improvements - Common Techniques (Continued)

Common Techniques	Usage
Process Modelling	Used to define business analysis processes and understand how to improve those processes to reduce problems from hand-offs, improve cycle times, or alter how business analysis work is performed to support improvements in downstream processes.
Reviews*	Used to identify changes to business analysis processes and deliverables that can be incorporated into future work.
Risk Analysis & Management*	Used to identify and manage potential conditions or events that may impact business analysis performance.
Root Cause Analysis	Used to help identify the underlying cause of failures or difficulties in accomplishing business analysis work.
Survey or Questionnaire	Used to gather feedback from stakeholders about their satisfaction with business analysis activities and deliverables.
Workshops	Used to gather assessments of business analysis performance and generate ideas for improvement opportunities.

* Typically used by those from Skilled through Strategist. Others may use them with varying degrees of adeptness, independence or understanding, as illustrated by the performance expectations for each of the subsequent lower levels.

4 Elicitation and Collaboration

4.1 Prepare for Elicitation

Definition

The purpose of Prepare for Elicitation is to effectively prepare for the elicitation activities.

Proficiency Descriptors

For descriptions on what each of the five levels mean, refer to the Proficiency Levels Legend.

5 - Strategist

- Create elicitation support material templates for others to use.
- Develop approaches and tactics for developing greater organizational understanding.
- Continually monitor processes, seeking opportunities for improvement.
- Develop and proactively drive adoption of innovative techniques, tools and templates for personal planning and organization.
- Foster a collaborative approach to encourage feedback, opinions and acceptance towards the use of elicitation tools and templates for personal planning and organization.
- Have been sought for advice, support and training by others on ways to effectively prepare for elicitation.
- Quickly understand team capabilities and skill/knowledge gaps.

- Develop nontraditional ideas for elicitation preparation.
- Create innovative ways of performing this task using common techniques.
- Demonstrate Expert Proficiency Descriptors.

4 - Expert

- Consistently prepare for complex elicitation activities.
- Support materials used are recognized as being "best practice".
- Apply insight and business acumen when connecting concepts as they relate to different aspects of the enterprise.
- Evaluate what worked in previous elicitation activities, what did not, and what could be done differently next time.
- Anticipate possible delays and proactively ask for assistance in reprioritizing.
- Work with large or multiple teams that span functions, issues, locations, and time zones to:
  - coordinate roles, responsibilities and interdependencies of all team members, and
  - show and promote respect for differences and diversity.
- Use a wide variety of sources to self-assess strengths/weaknesses.
- Support others with complex elicitation activities.
- Have been recognized internally as an authority in planning elicitation activities, and
  - have been frequently engaged by peers for support.
- Guide others on how to effectively use common techniques.
- Demonstrate Skilled Proficiency Descriptors.

3 - Skilled

- Understand the scope of the elicitation effort.
- Select appropriate elicitation techniques for the stakeholders.
- Set up logistics for elicitation activities.
- Prepare supporting materials.
- Prepare stakeholders in advance of elicitation sessions to ensure activities run smoothly and everyone works toward a common goal using methods such as:
  - gaining agreement for required stakeholder commitments,
  - monitoring stakeholder engagement and collaboration, and
  - demonstrating collaborative relationships with key stakeholders.
- Organize activities and manage time efficiently to consistently adhere to commitments and changing priorities.

- Analyze and use a holistic view of people, processes and technology to understand the enterprise.

- Adapt to and embrace changing situations as an opportunity rather than as an obstacle.

- Demonstrate an ability to learn quickly and willingly.

- Teach and ensure comprehension of new concepts involved in elicitation activities.

- Use common techniques.

2 - Practical Knowledge

- Can independently prepare for simple elicitation activities; relies on support from others in more complex situations.

- Rely on others to manage elicitation activity logistics.

- Have a basic knowledge of, and can follow, instructions for common techniques.

1 - General Awareness

- Have an understanding of the components involved in preparing for elicitation activities with support from others.

- Have an awareness of common techniques.

Common Techniques

Table 4.1.1: Prepare for Elicitation - Common Techniques

Common Techniques	Usage
Brainstorming	Used to collaboratively identify and reach consensus about which sources of business analysis information should be consulted and which elicitation techniques might be most effective.
Collaborative Games	Used to stimulate teamwork and collaboration by temporarily immersing participants in a safe and fun situation in which they can share their knowledge and experience on a given topic, identify hidden assumptions, and explore that knowledge in ways that may not occur during the course of normal interactions.
Data Mining	Used to identify information or patterns that require further investigation.
Document Analysis	Used to identify and assess candidate sources of supporting materials.

Table 4.1.1: Prepare for Elicitation - Common Techniques (Continued)

Common Techniques	Usage
Estimation	Used to estimate the time and effort required for the elicitation and the associated cost.
Interviews	Used to identify concerns about the planned elicitation, and can be used to seek authority to proceed with specific options.
Mind Mapping*	Used to collaboratively identify and reach consensus about which sources of business analysis information should be consulted and which elicitation techniques might be most effective.
Risk Analysis & Management*	Used to: • identify, assess, and manage conditions or situations that could disrupt the elicitation or affect the quality and validity of the elicitation results (the plans for the elicitation should be adjusted to avoid, transfer, or mitigate the most serious risks), and • identify and manage risks as they relate to stakeholder involvement, participation, and engagement.
Stakeholder List, Map, or Personas	Used to: • determine who should be consulted while preparing for the elicitation, who should participate in the event, and the appropriate roles for each stakeholder, and • determine who is available to participate in the business analysis work, show the informal relationshipsbetweenstakeholders, andunderstandwhichstakeholders should be consulted about different kinds of business analysis information.

* Typically used by those from Skilled through Strategist. Others may use them with varying degrees of adeptness, independence or understanding, as illustrated by the performance expectations for each of the subsequent lower levels.

4.2   Conduct Elicitation

Definition

The purpose of Conduct Elictation is to elicit (draw out, explore, and identify) information relevant to the change.

Proficiency Descriptors

For descriptions on what each of the five levels mean, refer to the Proficiency Levels Legend.

5 - Strategist

- Engage others in a discussion where they share information that they are not willing to share with others individuals.
- Develop nontraditional ideas for elicitation techniques.
- Consistently find "common ground" between differing viewpoints.
- Define strategies and plans for influencing multiple decision makers.
- Continually monitor processes, seeking opportunities for improvement.
- Have been:
    - recognized by leadership as an authority in directing elicitation activities, and
    - frequently assigned to lead complex elicitation activities.
- Develop and proactively drive adoption of tools to help others adjust their communication style, and
    - provide examples for how to handle certain circumstances with the right messaging (i.e if they say this, do this, or are difficult stakeholders).
- Create innovative ways of performing this task using common techniques.
- Demonstrate Expert Proficiency Descriptors.

4 - Expert

- Lead others in elicitation activities.
- Consistently uncover emotional drivers of stakeholders and develop messaging accordingly.
- Take existing tools and techniques and apply them in new ways.
- Consistently use meeting management skills and tools to keep discussions focused and organized.
- Regularly present ideas or suggestions to stakeholders in persuasive terms according to known needs/wants/emotional drivers of the audience, and
    - apply logic and emotion.

- Alter interpersonal style to interact with and influence a highly diverse set of individuals and groups in a range of situations.

- Exercise receptiveness to nontraditional ways of learning ideas.

- Have been:

  - recognized by colleagues as an authority in managing elicitation activities, and

  - frequently engaged by peers for support.

- Guide others on how to effectively use common techniques.

- Demonstrate Skilled Proficiency Descriptors.

3 - Skilled

- Facilitate the elicitation activity.

- Capture elicitation outcomes.

- Adapt verbal and non-verbal communication style to the needs of the situation and the individual.

- Use active listening and discovery skills to understand "real" issues/needs and build rapport.

- Use facilitation skills to encourage participation from all attendees.

- Influence others to drive action.

- Put all the pieces together to elicit information relevant to the change.

- Demonstrate an ability to learn quickly and willingly.

- Adapt to and embrace changing situations as an opportunity, rather than an obstacle.

- Use common techniques.

2 - Practical Knowledge

- Can elicit information relevant to the change with support of others.

- Capture the outcomes of the elicitation activity.

- Have a basic knowledge of and able to follow instructions for common techniques.

1 - General Awareness

- Understand the importance of eliciting information relevant to the change.

- Have an awareness of common techniques.

Common Techniques

Table 4.2.1: Conduct Elicitation- Common Techniques

Common Techniques	Usage
Benchmarking & Market Analysis**	Used as a source of business analysis information by comparing a specific process, system, product, service, or structure with some external baseline, such as a similar organization or baseline provided by an industry association. Market analysis is used to determine what customers want and what competitors provide.
Brainstorming	Used to generate many ideas from a group of stakeholders in a short period, and to organize and prioritize those ideas.
Business Rules Analysis	Used to identify the rules that govern decisions in an organization and that define, constrain, or enable organizational operations.
Collaborative Games	Used to develop a better understanding of a problem or to stimulate creative solutions.
Concept Modelling	Used to identify key terms and ideas of importance and define the relationships between them
Data Mining	Used to identify relevant information and patterns.
Data Modelling	Used to understand entity relationships during elicitation.
Document Analysis	Used to review existing systems, contracts, business procedures and policies, standards, and regulations.
Focus Groups	Used to identify and understand ideas and attitudes from a group.
Interface Analysis	Used to understand the interaction, and characteristics of that interaction, between two entities, such as two systems, two organizations, or two people or roles.

Table 4.2.1: Conduct Elicitation- Common Techniques (Continued)

Common Techniques	Usage
Interviews	Used to ask questions of stakeholders to uncover needs, identify problems, or discover opportunities.
Mind Mapping*	Used to generate many ideas from a group of stakeholders in a short period, and to organize and prioritize those ideas.
Observation	Used to gain insight about how work is currently done, possibly in different locations and in different circumstances.
Process Analysis	Used to understand current processes and to identify opportunities for improvement in those processes.
Process Modelling	Used to elicit processes with stakeholders during elicitation activities.
Prototyping	Used to elicit and validate stakeholders' needs through an iterative process that creates a model of requirements or designs.
Survey or Questionnaire	Used to elicit business analysis information, including information about customers, products, work practices, and attitudes, from a group of people in a structured way and in a relatively short period of time.
Workshops	Used to elicit business analysis information, including information about customers, products, work practices, and attitudes, from a group of people in a collaborative, facilitated way.

* Typically used by those from Skilled through Strategist. Others may use them with varying degrees of adeptness, independence or understanding, as illustrated by the performance expectations for each of the subsequent lower levels.

** Typically used by those from Expert through Strategist. Others may use them with varying degree of adeptness, independence or understanding, as illustrated by the performance expectations for each of the subsequent lower levels.

4.3 Confirm Elicitation Results

Definition

The purpose of Confirm Elicitation Results is to validate information with stakeholders for accuracy and consistency.

Proficiency Descriptors

For descriptions on what each of the five levels mean, refer to the Proficiency Levels Legend.

5 - Strategist

- Develop an approach for the current initiative to assess newly elicited results with source information and against other elicitation results.
- Create new methods for locating data and how to analyze its accuracy, importance, and validity.
- Debate issues to bring the most critical points to the forefront for decision making.
- Anticipate objections and proactively overcome them with data before the objection arises.
- Routinely perform scenario planning and exercise due diligence when validating information.
- Create innovative ways of performing this task using common techniques.
- Demonstrate Expert Proficiency Descriptors

4 - Expert

- Consistently validate complex information in an easy-to-understand manner.
- Identify potential gaps in elicitation results that may require additional elicitation activities.
- Engage all stakeholders and gain consensus in agreement of results.
- Present information based on audience's known preferences and needs/wants.
- Demonstrate foresight to uncover and resolve issues before they arise, and therefore rarely need to escalate them.
- Coach others on applying active listening and discovery skills.
- Guide others on how to effectively use common techniques.
- Demonstrate Skilled Proficiency Descriptors.

3 - Skilled

- Compare elicitation results against source information and other elicitation results.

- Validate that the elicitation results match the intention of stakeholder needs.

- Make and help others make the best decision based on appropriate criteria, such as:

  - business need,

  - opportunities,

  - risk,

  - compliance, and

  - the ability to achieve the desired outcome.

- Adapt verbal and non-verbal communication style to the needs of the situation and the individual.

- Use active listening and discovery skills to understand "real" issues/needs and build rapport.

- Influence others to drive action.

- Resolve conflicts and negotiate to reach agreements.

- Demonstrate well prepared, stakeholder-focused written communication.

- Use common techniques.

2 - Practical Knowledge

- Validate information with stakeholders with guidance from others.

- Have a basic knowledge of, and can follow, instructions for common techniques.

1 - General Awareness

- Understand the importance of validating information with stakeholders.

- Have an awareness of common techniques.

Common Techniques

Table 4.3.1: Confirm Elicitation Results - Common Techniques

Common Techniques	Usage
Document Analysis	Used to confirm elicitation results against source information or other existing documents.
Interviews	Used to: • confirm the business analysis information and to confirm that the integration of that information is correct, and • individually communicate information to stakeholders.
Reviews*	Used to: • confirm a set of elicitation results. Such reviews could be informal or formal depending on the risks of not having correct, useful, and relevant information, and • provide stakeholders with an opportunity to express feedback, request required adjustments, understand required responses and actions, and agree or provide approvals. Reviews can be used during group or individual collaboration.

Table 4.3.1: Confirm Elicitation Results - Common Techniques (Continued)

Common Techniques	Usage
Workshops	Used to: • conduct reviews of the drafted elicitation results using any level of formality (a predetermined agenda, scripts, or scenario tests may be used to walk through the elicitation results, and feedback is requested from the participants and recorded), and • provide stakeholders with an opportunity to express feedback and to understand required adjustments, responses, and actions., and • gain consensus and provide approvals (typically used during group collaboration).

* Typically used by those from Skilled through Strategist. Others may use them with varying degrees of adeptness, independence or understanding, as illustrated by the performance expectations for each of the subsequent lower levels.

4.4 Communicate Business Analysis Information

Definition

The purpose of Communicate Business Analysis Information to provide relevant information to stakeholders in a timely manner.

Proficiency Descriptors

For descriptions on what each of the five levels mean, refer to the Proficiency Levels Legend.

5 - Strategist

• Develop a repeatable approach for others to use for communicating business analysis information.

• Recognized as an authority on how to customize messaging to various levels of an organization.

• Foster collaborative approach to collect feedback, opinions, and acceptance towards the adoption of new approaches to communicate business analysis information.

• Create innovative ways of performing this task using common techniques.

• Demonstrate Expert Proficiency Descriptors.

4 - Expert

- Test and verify that relevant stakeholders understand the business analysis information.

- Consistently communicate complex information in an easy-to-understand manner.

- Have been recognized internally as an authority in dissemination of clear information, tailored to stakeholder needs.

- Regularly present ideas or suggestions to stakeholders in persuasive terms according to known needs/wants/emotional drivers of the audience, and

  - apply logic and emotion.

- Use a structured technique for enabling stakeholder-focused written communication, and

  - document profiles of each stakeholder, then update them as new insight is obtained.

- Guide others on how to effectively use common techniques.

- Demonstrate Skilled Proficiency Descriptors

3 - Skilled

- Obtain acknowledgement that stakeholders have a shared understanding of business analysis information.

- Determine objectives and format of communication.

- Use different methods to document and communicate information, based on stakeholder level of involvement and needs.

- Communicate the appropriate level of detail so stakeholders can understand the information

- Provide the forums for stakeholders to ask questions and/or raise any concerns.

- Feedback and opinions are openly shared by stakeholders about business analysis information.

- Adapt verbal and non-verbal communication style to the needs of the situation and the individual.

- Influence others to drive action.

- Resolve conflicts and negotiate to reach agreements.

- Demonstrate well prepared, stakeholder-focused written communication.

- Use active listening and discovery skills to understand "real" issues/needs and build rapport.

- Use common techniques.

2 - Practical Knowledge

- Communicate straight forward information with stakeholders, and
  - require support for more complex information or when potential issues may arise.
- Have a basic knowledge of, and can follow, instructions for common techniques.

1 - General Awareness

- Understand the importance of communicating information with stakeholders.
- Have an awareness of common techniques.

Common Techniques

Table 4.4.1: Communicate Business Analysis Information - Common Techniques

Common Techniques	Usage
Interviews	Used to: • confirm the business analysis information and to confirm that the integration of that information is correct, and • individually communicate information to stakeholders.
Reviews*	Used to: • confirm a set of elicitation results. (such reviews could be informal or formal depending on the risks of not having correct, useful, and relevant information), and • provide stakeholders with an opportunity to express feedback, request required adjustments, understand required responses and actions, and agree or provide approvals. Reviews can be used during group or individual collaboration.
Workshops	Used to provide stakeholders with an opportunity to express feedback and to understand required adjustments, responses, and actions. Workshops are also useful for gaining consensus and providing approvals (typically used during group collaboration).

* Typically used by those from Skilled through Strategist. Others may use them with varying degrees of adeptness, independence or understanding, as illustrated by the performance expectations for each of the subsequent lower levels.

4.5   Manage Stakeholder Collaboration

Definition

The purpose of Manage Stakeholder Collaboration is to effectively work with stakeholders to ensure delivery of required outcomes.

Proficiency Descriptors

For descriptions on what each of the five levels mean, refer to the Proficiency Levels Legend.

5 - Strategist

- Have been recognized by leadership as an authority in enhancing collaborative relationships with stakeholders at all levels of the organization.

- Consistently maintain enriched relationships with stakeholders.

- Foster a collaborative approach to collect ongoing feedback and opinions with stakeholders at all levels of the organization.

- Create support material templates for others to adopt.

- Create innovative ways of performing this task using common techniques.

- Demonstrate Expert Proficiency Descriptors.

4 - Expert

- Support others in complex stakeholder collaboration situations.

- Consistently gains agreement on commitments with stakeholders.

- Have established stakeholder engagement monitoring practices which are revered by colleagues.

- Have been:

  - recognized internally as an authority in stakeholder collaboration, and

  - frequently engaged by peers for support.

- Guide others on how to effectively use common techniques.

- Demonstrate Skilled Proficiency Descriptors.

3 - Skilled

- Set stakeholder expectations to ensure activities will run smoothly and they work toward a common goal.

- Gain agreement for required stakeholder commitments.

- Monitor stakeholder engagement and collaboration to:
    - assess stakeholders' level of participation and focus, and
    - raise attention to high risk behavior (such as diversion to other work, delayed approvals, or lack of involvement).
- Demonstrate collaborative relationships with key stakeholders to:
    - encourage the free-flow exchange of information, ideas, or innovation, and
    - promote an atmosphere of shared effort to resolve problems and achieve desired outcomes.
- Analyze and use a holistic view of people, processes and technology to understand the enterprise.
- Adapt to and embrace changing situations as an opportunity, rather than an obstacle.
- Organize activities and manage time efficiently in order to consistently adhere to commitments and changing priorities.
- Teach and ensure comprehension of new concepts.
- Demonstrate an ability to learn quickly and willingly.
- Resolve conflicts and negotiate to obtain agreement.
- Encourage teamwork by working in collaboration with others to achieve goals and objectives.
- Use common techniques.

2 - Practical Knowledge

- Can independently manage stakeholder collaboration in simple situations and rely on support from others in more involved situations.
- Rely on others to gain agreement on commitments.
- Have a basic knowledge of, and can follow, instructions for common techniques.

1 - General Awareness

- Have an understanding of the components involved in managing stakeholder collaboration.
- Have an awareness of common techniques.

Common Techniques

Table 4.5.1: Manage Stakeholder Collaboration - Common Techniques

Common Techniques	Usage
Collaborative Games	Used to stimulate teamwork and collaboration by temporarily immersing participants in a safe and fun situation in which they can share their knowledge and experience on a given topic, identify hidden assumptions, and explore that knowledge in ways that may not occur during the course of normal interactions.
Lessons Learned	Used to understand stakeholders' satisfaction or dissatisfaction, and offer them an opportunity to help improve the working relationships.
Risk Analysis & Management*	Used to identify and manage risks as they relate to stakeholder involvement, participation, and engagement.
Stakeholder Lists, Maps, or Personas	Used to determine who is available to participate in the business analysis work, show the informal relationships between stakeholders, and understand which stakeholders should be consulted about different kinds of business analysis information.

* Typically used by those from Skilled through Strategist. Others may use them with varying degrees of adeptness, independence or understanding, as illustrated by the performance expectations for each of the subsequent lower levels.

5 Requirements Life Cycle Management

5.1   Trace Requirements

Definition

The purpose of Trace Requirements is to ensure that requirements and designs at different levels are aligned, and that changes are effectively managed.

Proficiency Descriptors

For descriptions on what each of the five levels mean, refer to the Proficiency Levels Legend.

5 - Strategist

- Develop and drive adoption of tools, templates, and/or processes for aligning requirements and design.

- Create innovative ways to use the common techniques to perform this task, such as Functional Decomposition.

- Develop an innovative approach for using new tools, templates and processes that:

    - explain the rationale for adoption, and

    - invite intentional feedback and opinions from others.

- Develop and drive adoption of new methodologies as appropriate, and develop tools, templates, and processes to support them.

- Have been recognized as a visionary in:

  - aligning requirements and designs, resulting in requests from leadership to lead related complex change initiatives, and

  - mastery of several business analysis tools, resulting in frequent engagement by peers for support in using them.

- Demonstrate Expert Proficiency Descriptors.

4 - Expert

- Consistently align complex requirements with design independently.

- Have been recognized as an authority in several analysis methodologies, and as a result:

  - have been asked by leadership to spearhead change in methodologies, and

  - have been asked by peers for advice and support.

- Recognized by colleagues as an authority in aligning requirements and designs, and frequently engaged by peers for support.

- Coach others on:

  - traceability relationships, and

  - effective use of business analysis tools.

- Invite recommendations from others to conduct effective requirements traceability.

- Guide others on how to use common techniques effectively.

- Demonstrate Skilled Proficiency Descriptors.

3 - Skilled

- Consider value and relationships while tracing requirements.

- Identify the relationships to track to effectively manage traceability.

- Leverage appropriate business analysis tools to align requirements and designs and effectively manage changes.

- Demonstrate capability in multiple analysis methodologies.

- Put all the pieces together to align requirements and designs and effectively manage changes.

- Ensure approaches used to trace requirement relationships are acceptable norms by stakeholders.

- Use common techniques to assist in the execution of this task.

2 - Practical Knowledge

- Participate in the traceability activities.
- Have a basic knowledge of, and can follow, instructions for common techniques.

1 - General Awareness

- Understand the need to ensure that requirements and designs align with one another through traceability.
- Have an awareness of common techniques.

Common Techniques

Table 5.1.1: Trace Requirements- Common Techniques

Common Techniques	Usage
Business Rules Analysis	Used to trace business rules to requirements that they support, or rules that support requirements.
Functional Decomposition	Used to break down solution scope into smaller components for allocation, as well as to trace high-level concepts to low-level concepts.
Process Modelling	Used to visually show the future state process, as well as tracing requirements to the future state process.
Scope Modelling	Used to visually depict scope, as well as trace requirements to the area of scope the requirement supports.

5.2   Maintain Requirements

Definition

The purpose of Maintain Requirements is to identify and maintain requirements and designs for reuse by ensuring accuracy and consistency.

Proficiency Descriptors

For descriptions on what each of the five levels mean, refer to the Proficiency Levels Legend.

5 - Strategist

- Develop and drive adoption of an archival system that stores historical requirements and how they were implemented.

- Develop training materials and "tips" that stakeholders can leverage to improve their efficiency in using business analysis tools.

- Capture best practices and broadcast them to the business analysis community.

- Create innovative ways of performing this task using common techniques.

- Demonstrate Expert Proficiency Descriptors.

4 - Expert

- Share requirements/designs to identify overlaps and trends with stakeholders.

- Share change and improvement strategies for existing and future projects with colleagues.

- Consistently synthesize complex data from disparate sources and understand how they impact the enterprise or organization.

- Consistently identify and leverage the appropriate business analysis tools based on the requirements and purpose of the task.

- Frequently engaged by peers for advice and support.

- Guide others on how to effectively use common techniques.

- Demonstrate Skilled Proficiency Descriptors.

3 - Skilled

- Maintain requirements so they remain correct and current after an approved change.

- Ensure that the content and intent of the requirement is maintained.

- Ensure approaches used to maintain requirements are understood by stakeholders.

- Manage requirements and attributes so they can be easily stored and accessed.

- Manage requirements in such a manner they can easily be reused in the future.

- Analyze and use a holistic view of people, processes and technology to understand the enterprise.

- Leverage appropriate business analysis tools to identify and maintain requirements and designs for reuse.

- Demonstrate an understanding of the organization's nuances and how to get things done.

- Use common techniques.

2 - Practical Knowledge

- Maintain requirements throughout the change, with support from others.

- Have a basic knowledge of, and can follow, instructions for common techniques.

1 - General Awareness

- Understand the importance of maintaining requirements and designs.

- Aware of common techniques.

Common Techniques

Table 5.2.1: Maintain Requirements - Common Techniques

Common Techniques	Usage
Business Rules Analysis	Used to identify business rules that may be similar across the enterprise in order to facilitate reuse.
Data Flow Diagrams	Used to identify information flow that may be similar across the enterprise in order to facilitate reuse.
Data Modelling	Used to identify data structure that may be similar across the enterprise in order to facilitate reuse.
Document Analysis	Used to analyze existing documentation about an enterprise that can serve as the basis for maintaining and reusing requirements.
Functional Decomposition	Used to identify requirements associated with the components and available for reuse.
Process Modelling	Used to identify requirements associated with the processes that may be available for reuse.
Use Cases and Scenarios	Used to identify a solution component that may be utilized by more than one solution.
User Stories	Used to identify requirements associated with the story that may be available for reuse.

5.3   Prioritize Requirements

Definition

The purpose of Prioritize Requirements is to rank requirements and designs according to relative importance.

Proficiency Descriptors

For descriptions on what each of the five levels mean, refer to the Proficiency Levels Legend.

5 - Strategist

- Demonstrate subject matter expertise in prioritization so that leaders grant the authority to resolve issues independently.

- Create new methods for locating data and how to analyze its accuracy and importance.

- Foster a collaborative approach to obtain feedback, opinions, and agreement on the adoption of new prioritization methods.

- Capture best practices in prioritization and broadcast them to the business analysis community.

- Always incorporate relevant product, service, business, and industry acumen in prioritization.

- Have been recognized by leadership as an authority in prioritizing requirements and designs, such that they:

  - frequently ask for input, and

  - typically implement recommendations.

- Create innovative ways of performing this task using common techniques.

- Demonstrate Expert Proficiency Descriptors.

4 - Expert

- Provide relevant data to support recommended prioritization decisions.

- Ensure stakeholders understanding and acceptance of prioritization decisions.

- Demonstrate foresight to uncover and resolve issues before they arise, and therefore rarely need to escalate them.

- Engage all stakeholders and gain consensus before pursuing a course of action.

- Help others understand the impact of prioritization on other business functions including strategy, financial, and legal.

- Have been:

  - recognized by colleagues as an authority in prioritizing requirements and designs, and

  - frequently engaged by peers for support

- Guide others on how to effectively use common techniques.

- Demonstrate Skilled Proficiency Descriptors.

3 - Skilled

- Ensure that the basis of prioritization is followed, as agreed upon by relevant stakeholders.

- Guide stakeholders through the challenges of prioritization.

- Re-evaluate priority with stakeholders as new information becomes available.

- Demonstrate the ability to incorporate business and industry knowledge into work

- Make and help others make the best decision based on appropriate criteria, such as:

  - business need,

  - opportunities,

  - risk,

  - compliance, and

  - the ability to achieve the desired outcome.

- Resolve conflicts and negotiate to reach agreements, during prioritization.

- Use common techniques.

2 - Practical Knowledge

- Can prioritize requirements/designs with support from others according to established practices.

- Have a basic knowledge of, and can follow, instructions for common techniques.

1 - General Awareness

- Understand the importance of prioritizing requirements/designs.

- Have an awareness of common techniques.

Common Techniques

Table 5.3.1: Prioritize Requirements- Common Techniques

Common Techniques	Usage
Backlog Management	Used to compare requirements to be prioritized. The backlog can be the location where the prioritization is maintained.
Business Cases*	Used to assess requirements against identified business goals and objectives to determine importance.
Decision Analysis	Used to identify high-value requirements.
Estimation	Used to produce estimates for the basis of prioritization.
Financial Analysis*	Used to assess the financial value of a set of requirements and how the timing of delivery will affect that value.
Interviews	Used to gain an understanding of a single or small group of stakeholders' basis of prioritization or priorities.
Item Tracking	Used to track issues raised by stakeholders during prioritization.
Prioritization	Used to facilitate the process of prioritization.
Risk Analysis & Management	Used to understand the risks for the basis of prioritization.
Workshops	Used to gain an understanding of stakeholders' basis of prioritization or priorities in a facilitated group setting.

* Typically used by those from Skilled through Strategist. Others may use them with varying degrees of adeptness, independence or understanding, as illustrated by the performance expectations for each of the subsequent lower levels.

5.4   Assess Requirements Changes

Definition

The purpose of Assess Requirements Changes is to evaluate the impact of proposed changes to requirements and designs.

Proficiency Descriptors

For descriptions on what each of the five levels mean, refer to the Proficiency Levels Legend.

5 - Strategist

- Create new ways to assess the possibilities of a situation resulting from changes to requirements and designs.

- Apply foresight when connecting concepts to enterprise components.

- Develop an innovative approach for using new tools, templates and processes that:

  - explain the rationale for adoption, and

  - invite intentional feedback and opinions from others.

- Develop a network of Subject Matter Experts (SMEs) inside and outside of the organization in order to:

  - contribute knowledge/skill into the network, and

  - draw knowledge/skill from the network appropriately.

- Have been recognized by leadership as an authority in evaluating the impact of proposed changes to requirements and designs, such that they:

  - frequently ask for input, and

  - typically implement recommendations.

- Create innovative ways of performing this task using common techniques.

- Demonstrate Expert Proficiency Descriptors.

4 - Expert

- Consistently guide complex impact resolutions activities.

- Perform complex impact assessments of changes to requirements and designs.

- Consistently synthesize complex data from disparate sources and understand how they impact the enterprise or organization.

- Use supporting data to challenge any changes with negative impacts.

- Foster a collaborative approach to obtain feedback, opinions, and acceptance during assessments of changes to requirements and design.

- Frequently engaged by peers for advice and support on evaluating impact of proposed changes to requirements and designs.

- Coach others how to use the input from all stakeholders to make the most informed decisions.

- Guide others on how to effectively use common techniques.

- Demonstrate Skilled Proficiency Descriptors.

3 - Skilled

- Regularly monitor the impact of changes to requirements and designs, and use historical data to evaluate the potential impact of current proposed changes.

- Execute the defined change control process.

- Complete impact analysis activities, as needed.

- Facilitate impact resolution activities.

- Demonstrate an understanding of the organization's nuances and how to get things done

- Analyze and use a holistic view of people, processes and technology to understand the enterprise.

- Make and help others make the best decision based on appropriate criteria, such as:

  - business need,

  - opportunities,

  - risk,

  - compliance, and

  - the ability to achieve the desired outcome.

- Use common techniques.

2 - Practical Knowledge

- Evaluate the impact of proposed changes to requirements/designs with support from others.

- Have a basic knowledge of, and can follow, instructions for common techniques.

1 - General Awareness

- Understand the importance of evaluating the impact of proposed changes to requirements/designs.

- Have an awareness of common techniques.

Common Techniques

Table 5.4.1: Assess Requirements Changes- Common Techniques

Common Techniques	Usage
Business Cases*	Used to justify a proposed change.
Business Rules Analysis	Used to assess changes to business policies and business rules, and develop revised guidance.
Decision Analysis	Used to facilitate the change assessment process.
Estimation	Used to determine the size of the change.
Financial Analysis*	Used to estimate the financial consequences of a proposed change.
Interface Analysis	Used to help business analysts identify interfaces that can be affected by the change
Interviews	Used to gain an understanding of the impact on the organization or its assets from a single or small group of stakeholders.
Item Tracking	Used to track any issues or conflicts discovered during impact analysis.
Risk Analysis & Management*	Used to determine the level of risk associated with the change.
Workshops	Used to gain an understanding of the impact or to resolve changes in a group setting.

*Typically used by those from Skilled through Strategist. Others may use them with varying degrees of adeptness, independence or understanding, as illustrated by the performance expectations for each of the subsequent lower levels.

5.5   Approve Requirements

Definition

The purpose of Approve Requirements is to obtain agreement on and approval of requirements and designs for business analysis work.

Proficiency Descriptors

For descriptions on what each of the five levels mean, refer to the Proficiency Levels Legend.

5 - Strategist

- Deal with unforeseen issues effectively by:

  - assembling and/or developing resources, processes and tools,

  - developing a go-to network of empowered people and resources who are quick to respond,

  - demonstrating subject matter expertise in obtaining agreement and approval of requirements and designs, and

  - attaining authority from leadership to enact resolution independently.

- Engage others in a discussion where they share information that they are not willing to share with other individuals.

- Have been recognized by leadership as an authority in obtaining agreement on requirements and designs for business analysis work, and being frequently assigned to manage complex business analysis work.

- Create innovative ways of performing this task using common techniques.

- Demonstrate Expert Proficiency Descriptors.

4 - Expert

- Consistently resolve complex issues and conflicts independently and lead others in this task.

- Consistently uncover emotional drivers of stakeholders and develop messaging accordingly.

- Help others overcome their unforeseen issues.

- Coach others on applying active listening and discovery skills to understand real issues/needs and build rapport.

- Guide others on how to effectively use common techniques.

- Demonstrate Skilled Proficiency Descriptors.

3 - Skilled

- Understand stakeholder roles and authority levels in approving requirements and designs.
- Manage conflicts and resolve issues that arise, during the approval process.
- Use appropriate methods to gain consensus about key business analysis information.
- Track and communicate approval and implementation decisions for requirements and designs.
- Maintain audit history of changes to requirements and designs.
- Adapt verbal and non-verbal communication style to the needs of the situation and the individual.
- Use active listening and discovery skills to understand "real" issues/needs and build rapport.
- Resolve conflicts and negotiate to reach agreements.
- Use common techniques.

2 - Practical Knowledge

- Obtain approval of requirements and designs with support from others.
- Have a basic knowledge of, and can follow, instructions for common techniques.

1 - General Awareness

- Understand the importance of obtaining agreement on requirements and designs.
- Have an awareness of common techniques.

Common Techniques

Table 5.5.1: Approve Requirements - Common Techniques

Common Techniques	Usage
Acceptance and Evaluation Criteria	Used to define approval criteria.
Decision Analysis	Used to resolve issues and gain agreement.
Item Tracking	Used to track issues identified during the agreement process.
Reviews*	Used to evaluate requirements.
Workshops	Used to facilitate obtaining approval.

*Typically used by those from Skilled through Strategist. Others may use them with varying degrees of adeptness, independence or understanding, as illustrated by the performance expectations for each of the subsequent lower levels.

6 Strategy Analysis

6.1   Analyze Current State

Definition

The purpose of Analyze Current State is to understand the reasons for change and what will be impacted by the change.

Proficiency Descriptors

For descriptions on what each of the five levels mean, refer to the Proficiency Levels Legend.

5 - Strategist

- Apply foresight when connecting concepts to enterprise components.

- Apply foresight to predict external drivers for change, and draw from experience to recommend how to address them.

- Develop a network of Subject Matter Experts (SMEs) inside and outside of the organization and do the following:

  - contribute knowledge/skill into the network, and

  - draw knowledge/skill from the network appropriately.

- Create innovative ways of performing this task using common techniques.

- Demonstrate Expert Proficiency Descriptors.

4 - Expert

- Consistently define business needs so that they:
  - can be resolved,
  - are easy to understand (complex needs are explained and stated simply), and
  - are actionable.
- Apply insight and business acumen when connecting concepts as they relate to different aspects of the enterprise
- Research, analyze and synthesize data to support rationale for change
- Help others see the value of the change with actions such as:
  - customizing the explanation/justification according to the emotional drivers of the stakeholder(s), and
  - soliciting and incorporate feedback from stakeholders.
- Have been frequently engaged by peers for advice and support in understanding the rationale for change and what will be impacted by the change.
- Coach others on the importance of using relevant business acumen and industry knowledge in all communications with stakeholders and other team members.
- Guide others on how to effectively use common techniques.
- Demonstrate Skilled Proficiency Descriptors.

3 - Skilled

- Identify and define the real business needs.
- Demonstrate an understanding of the organization's nuances and how to get things done.
- Understand the organization's:
  - capabilities and processes,
  - utilized technology and infrastructure,
  - policies and business rules,
  - business architecture, and
  - internal assets.
- Understand external influencers.
- Demonstrate the ability to incorporate business and industry knowledge into work.

- Analyze and use a holistic view of people, processes and technology to understand the enterprise.

- Use common techniques.

2 - Practical Knowledge

- Understand some, but not all, of the factors that influence/determine the need for change.

- Define business needs with support of others.

- Have a basic knowledge of, and can follow, instructions for common techniques.

1 - General Awareness

- Understand the importance of analyzing the environment associated with the change.

- Have an awareness of common techniques.

Common Techniques

Table 6.1.1: Analyze Current State - Common Techniques

Common Techniques	Usage
Benchmarking & Market Analysis**	Used to provide an understanding of where there are opportunities for improvement in the current state. Specific frameworks that may be useful include 5 Forces analysis, PEST, STEEP, CATWOE, and others.
Business Capability Analysis**	Used to identify gaps, and prioritize them in relation to value and risk.
Business Cases*	Used to capture information regarding the business need and opportunity.
Business Model Canvas**	Used to: - provide an understanding of the value proposition that the enterprise satisfies for its customers, the critical factors in delivering that value, and the resulting cost and revenue streams, and - help understand the context for any change and identify the problems and opportunities that may have the most significant impact.

Table 6.1.1: Analyze Current State - Common Techniques (Continued)

Common Techniques	Usage
Concept Modelling	Used to capture key terms and concepts in the business domain and define the relationships between them.
Data Mining	Used to obtain information on the performance of the enterprise.
Document Analysis	Used to analyze any existing documentation about the current state, including (but not limited to): <ul><li>documents created during the implementation of a solution,</li><li>training manuals,</li><li>issue reports,</li><li>competitor information,</li><li>supplier agreements,</li><li>published industry benchmarks,</li><li>published technology trends, and</li><li>performance metrics.</li></ul>
Financial Analysis*	Used to understand the profitability of the current state and the financial capability to deliver change.
Focus Groups	Used to solicit feedback from customers or end users about the current state.
Functional Decomposition	Used to break down complex systems or relationships in the current state.
Interviews	Used to facilitate dialogue with stakeholders to understand the current state and any needs evolving from the current state.
Item Tracking	Used to track and manage issues discovered about the current state.
Lessons Learned	Used to enable the assessment of failures and opportunities for improvement in past initiatives, which may drive a business need for process improvement.
Metrics and Key Performance Indicators (KPIs)	Used to assess the performance of the current state of an enterprise.

Table 6.1.1: Analyze Current State - Common Techniques (Continued)

Common Techniques	Usage
Mind Mapping*	Used to explore relevant aspects of the current state and better understand relevant factors affecting the business need.
Observation	Used to provide opportunities for insights into needs within the current state that have not been identified previously by a stakeholder.
Organizational Modelling	Used to describe the roles, responsibilities, and reporting structures that exist within the current state organization.
Process Analysis	Used to identify opportunities to improve the current state.
Risk Analysis & Management*	Used to identify risks to the current state.
Root Cause Analysis	Used to provide an understanding of the underlying causes of any problems in the current state in order to further clarify a need.
Scope Modelling	Used to help define the boundaries on the current state description.
Survey or Questionnaire	Used to help gain an understanding of the current state from a large, varied, or disparate group of stakeholders.
SWOT Analysis	Used to evaluate the strengths, weaknesses, opportunities, and threats to the current state enterprise.
Vendor Assessment**	Used to determine whether any vendors that are part of the current state are adequately meeting commitments, or if any changes are needed.
Workshops	Used to engage stakeholders to collaboratively describe the current state and their needs.

* Typically used by those from Skilled through Strategist. Others may use them with varying degrees of adeptness, independence or understanding, as illustrated by the performance expectations for each of the subsequent lower levels.

** Typically used by those from Expert through Strategist. Others may use them with varying degree of adeptness, independence or understanding, as illustrated by the performance expectations for each of the subsequent lower levels.

6.2   Define Future State

Definition

The purpose of Define Future State is to determine the set of necessary conditions to meet the business need.

Proficiency Descriptors

For descriptions on what each of the five levels mean, refer to the Proficiency Levels Legend.

5 - Strategist

- Consistently influence business policies and practices.
- Develop approaches and tactics for developing greater organizational understanding.
- Create new ways to identify all potential alternatives to address business needs.
- Develop an innovative approach for using new tools, templates and processes that:
  - explain the rationale for adoption, and
  - invite intentional feedback and opinions from others.
- Develop a network of Subject Matter Experts (SMEs) inside and outside of the organization and do the following:
  - contribute knowledge/skill into the network, and
  - draw knowledge/skill from the network appropriately.
- Have been:
  - recognized by leadership as an authority in determining the conditions to meet the business need, and
  - frequently assigned complex business needs to satisfy.
- Create innovative ways of performing this task using common techniques.
- Demonstrate Expert Proficiency Descriptors.

4 - Expert

- Consistently synthesize complex data from disparate sources and understand how they impact the enterprise or organization.
- Ensure the elements of future state support one another, meet business goals and objectives, and integrate with the future state of the enterprise.

- Use a structured approach for creative solutions to complex problems.

- Develop a network of SMEs within the organization.

- Have been:

  - recognized by colleagues as an authority in determining the conditions to meet the business need, and

  - frequently asked by peers for support.

- Guide others on how to effectively use common techniques.

- Demonstrate Skilled Proficiency Descriptors.

3 - Skilled

- Articulate business goals and objectives.

- Determine the solution scope.

- Identify:

  - constraints,

  - potential changes to organizational structure and culture required to support the desired change,

  - new or modified capabilities and business processes that will be required to support the change,

  - new or modified technology and infrastructure that will be required to support the change

  - new or modified organizational policies and business rules required to support the change, and

  - assumptions related to the future state.

- Assess resource alignment for future state and transition to future state.

- Evaluate the potential value for the future state.

- Demonstrate an understanding of the organization's nuances and how to get things done.

- Analyze and use a holistic view of people, processes and technology to understand the enterprise.

- Think creatively and help others to think creatively to identify innovative solutions.

- Use common techniques.

2 - Practical Knowledge

- Can participate in activities to define the necessary conditions to meet the business need, with clear direction from others.

- Have a basic knowledge of, and can follow, instructions for common techniques.

1 - General Awareness

- Understand the importance of determining the conditions required to meet business needs.

- Have an awareness of common techniques.

Common Techniques

Table 6.2.1: Define Future State - Common Techniques

Common Techniques	Usage
Acceptance and Evaluation Criteria	Used to identify what may make the future state acceptable and/or how options may be evaluated.
Balanced Scorecard	Used to set targets for measuring the future state.
Benchmarking & Market Analysis**	Used to make decisions about future state business objectives.
Brainstorming	Used to collaboratively come up with ideas for the future state.
Business Cases*	Used to capture the desired outcomes of the change initiative.
Business Model Canvas**	Used to plan strategy for the enterprise by mapping out the needed infrastructure, target customer base, financial cost structure, and revenue streams required to fulfill the value proposition to customers in the desired future state.
Decision Analysis	Used to compare the different future state options and understand which is the best choice.
Decision Modelling	Used to model complex decisions regarding future state options.
Financial Analysis	Used to estimate the potential financial returns to be delivered by a proposed future state.
Functional Decompositon	Used to break down complex systems within the future state for better understanding.

Table 6.2.1: Define Future State - Common Techniques (Continued)

Common Techniques	Usage
Interviews	Used to talk to stakeholders to understand their desired future state, which needs they want to address, and what desired business objectives they want to meet.
Lessons Learned	Used to determine which opportunities for improvement will be addressed and how the current state can be improved upon.
Metrics and Key Performance Indicators (KPIs)	Used to determine when the organization has succeeded in achieving the business objectives.
Mind Mapping*	Used to develop ideas for the future state and understand relationships between them.
Organizational Modelling	Used to describe the roles, responsibilities, and reporting structures that would exist within the future state organization.
Process Modelling	Used to describe how work would occur in the future state.
Prototyping	Used to model future state options and could also help determine potential value.
Scope Modelling	Used to define the boundaries of the enterprise in the future state.
Survey or Questionnaire	Used to understand stakeholders' desired future state, which needs they want to address, and what desired business objectives they want to meet.
SWOT Analysis	Used to evaluate the strengths, weaknesses, opportunities, and threats that may be exploited or mitigated by the future state.
Vendor Assessment**	Used to assess potential value provided by vendor solution options.
Workshops	Used to work with stakeholders to collaboratively describe the future state.

* Typically used by those from Skilled through Strategist. Others may use them with varying degrees of adeptness, independence or understanding, as illustrated by the performance expectations for each of the subsequent lower levels.

** Typically used by those from Expert through Strategist. Others may use them with varying degree of adeptness, independence or understanding, as illustrated by the performance expectations for each of the subsequent lower levels.

6.3   Assess Risks

Definition

The purpose of Assess Risks is to assess the undesirable consequences of transition to or of the final future state.

Proficiency Descriptors

For descriptions on what each of the five levels mean, refer to the Proficiency Levels Legend.

5 - Strategist

- Apply foresight to:
  - identify and overcome potential roadblocks that might lead to a negative consequence, and
  - predict what competitors will do, and how to counteract it.
- Develop and proactively drive adoption of tools, templates, and processes for risk analysis and management.
- Develop approaches and tactics for developing greater organizational understanding.
  - explain the rationale for adoption, and
  - invite intentional feedback and opinions from others.
- Create new ways to assess the possibilities of a situation.
- Consistently apply new ideas and foresight to anticipate and avoid issues.
- Have been:
  - recognized by leadership as an authority in preventing undesirable consequences while transitioning to the final future state, and
  - frequently assigned high visibility and/or complex projects.
- Create innovative ways of performing this task using common techniques.
- Demonstrate Expert Proficiency Descriptors.

4 - Expert

- Consistently define and mitigate undesirable consequences while transitioning to a final future state.

- Leverage historical data to assess the impact and likelihood of risks occurring for the current change.

- Foster a collaborative approach to gain feedback and acceptance to assess, manage, and mitigate risks.

- Apply insight and business acumen when connecting concepts as they relate to different aspects of the enterprise.

- Consistently apply risk models that are suitable to the situation.

- Use a structured approach for creative solutions to complex problems.

- Have been:

    - recognized by colleagues as an authority in preventing undesirable consequences while transitioning to the final future state, and

    - frequently asked by peers for support.

- Coach others on how to assess situations in order to make the most informed decisions about which course of action to pursue.

- Guide others on how to effectively use common techniques.

- Demonstrate Skilled Proficiency Descriptors.

3 - Skilled

- Identify unknowns.

- Identify and manage constraints, assumptions and dependencies.

- Quantify the impact of risk factors.

- Assess stakeholder and organizational risk tolerances.

- Recommend an effective course of action based on risk assessment.

- Demonstrate the ability to incorporate business and industry knowledge into work.

- Analyze and use a holistic view of people, processes and technology to understand the enterprise.

- Think creatively and help others to think creatively to identify innovative solutions.

- Make and help others make the best decision based on appropriate criteria, such as: business need, opportunities, risk, compliance and ability to achieve the desired outcome.

- Use common techniques.

2 - Practical Knowledge

- Can perform some, but not all, tasks required to avoid or mitigate negative consequences while transitioning to the future state.

- Can follow recommended courses of action provided by others.

- Have a basic knowledge of, and can follow, instructions for common techniques.

1 - General Awareness

- Understand the importance of avoiding or mitigating negative consequences while transitioning to the future state.

- Have an awareness of common techniques.

Common Techniques

Table 6.3.1: Assess Risks- Common Techniques

Common Techniques	Usage
Brainstorming	Used to collaboratively identify potential risks for assessment.
Business Cases*	Used to capture risks associated with alternative change strategies.
Decision Analysis*	Used to assess problems.
Document Analysis	Used to analyze existing documents for potential risks, constraints, assumptions, and dependencies.
Financial Analysis*	Used to understand the potential effect of risks on the financial value of the solution.
Interviews	Used to understand what stakeholders think might be risks and the various factors of those risks.
Lessons Learned	Used as a foundation of past issues that might be risks.
Mind Mapping*	Used to identify and categorize potential risks and understand their relationships.
Risk Analysis & Management*	Used to identify and manage risks.
Root Cause Analysis	Used to identify and address the underlying problem creating a risk.

Table 6.3.1: Assess Risks- Common Techniques (Continued)

Common Techniques	Usage
Survey or Questionnaire	Used to understand what stakeholders think might be risks and the various factors of those risks.
Workshops	Used to understand what stakeholders think might be risks and the various factors of those risks.

* Typically used by those from Skilled through Strategist. Others may use them with varying degrees of adeptness, independence or understanding, as illustrated by the performance expectations for each of the subsequent lower levels.

6.4   Define Change Strategy

Definition

The purpose of Define Change Strategy is to recommend an appropriate strategy for change after developing and assessing alternative approaches.

Proficiency Descriptors

For descriptions on what each of the five levels mean, refer to the Proficiency Levels Legend.

5 - Strategist

- Create and drive adoption of tools, templates, and processes for developing transition states.

- Develop metrics and a rating system for evaluating solutions.

- Develop approaches and tactics for developing greater organizational understanding.

- Develop and proactively drive adoption of new tools or templates for evaluating alternatives.

- Develop an innovative approach for using new tools, templates and processes that:

  - explain the rationale for adoption, and

  - invite intentional feedback and opinions from others.

- Capture change strategy best practices and broadcast them to the business analysis community.

- Create innovative ways of performing this task using common techniques.

- Demonstrate Expert Proficiency Descriptors.

4 - Expert

- Consistently develop effective change strategies, even for complex situations.

- Apply insight and business acumen when connecting concepts as they relate to different aspects of the enterprise.

- Engage all stakeholders and gain consensus before pursuing a course of action.

- Develop a network of SMEs within the organization.

- Have been:

  - recognized by colleagues as an authority in developing effective change strategies, and

  - frequently engaged by peers for support.

- Guide others on how to effectively use common techniques.

- Demonstrate Skilled Proficiency Descriptors.

3 - Skilled

- Define solution scope to understand which new capabilities the change will deliver.

- Perform gap analysis to understand missing or improved capabilities required for the change.

- Complete the enterprise readiness assessment.

- Develop an effective change strategy.

- Encourage feedback and acceptance of the change strategy from key stakeholders.

- Develop appropriate transition states and complete release plans.

- Demonstrate an understanding of the organization's nuances and how to get things done.

- Analyze and use a holistic view of people, processes and technology to understand the enterprise.

- Make and help others make the best decision based on appropriate criteria, such as:

  - business need,

  - opportunities,

  - risk,

  - compliance, and

  - the ability to achieve the desired outcome.

- Use common techniques.

2 - Practical Knowledge

- Can independently perform some, but not all, tasks required to develop and assess alternate approaches to change.

- Have a basic knowledge of, and can follow, instructions for common techniques.

1 - General Awareness

- Understand the importance of a change strategy.

- Have an awareness of the enterprise readiness assessment.

- Have an awareness of common techniques.

Common Techniques

Table 6.4.1: Define Change Strategy - Common Techniques

Common Techniques	Usage
Balanced Scorecard**	Used to define the metrics that will be used to evaluate the effectiveness of the change strategy.
Benchmarking & Market Analysis	Used to make decisions about which change strategy is appropriate.
Brainstorming	Used to collaboratively come up with ideas for change strategies.
Business Capability Analysis	Used to prioritize capability gaps in relation to value and risk.
Business Cases*	Used to capture information about the recommended change strategy and other potential strategies that were assessed but not recommended.
Business Model Canvas**	Used to define the changes needed in the current infrastructure, customer base, and financial structure of the organization in order to achieve the potential value.
Decision Analysis	Used to compare different change strategies and choose which is most appropriate.
Estimation	Used to determine timelines for activities within the change strategy.

Table 6.4.1: Define Change Strategy - Common Techniques (Continued)

Common Techniques	Usage
Financial Analysis*	Used to understand the potential value associated with a change strategy, and evaluate strategies against targets set for return on investments.
Focus Groups	Used to bring customers or end users together to solicit their input on the solution and change strategy.
Functional Decompostion	Used to break down the components of the solution into parts when developing a change strategy.
Interviews	Used to talk to stakeholders in order to fully describe the solution scope and change scope, and to understand their suggestions for a change strategy.
Lessons Learned	Used to understand what went wrong in past changes in order to improve this change strategy.
Mind Mapping*	Used to develop and explore ideas for change strategies.
Organizational Modelling	Used to describe the roles, responsibilities, and reporting structures that are necessary during the change and are part of the solution scope.
Process Modelling	Used to describe how work would occur in the solution scope or during the change.
Scope Modelling	Used to define the boundaries on the solution scope and change scope descriptions.
SWOT Analysis*	Used to make decisions about which change strategy is appropriate.
Vendor Assessment**	Used to determine whether any vendors are part of the change strategy, either to implement the change or to be part of the solution.
Workshops	Used in work with stakeholders to collaboratively develop change strategies.

* Typically used by those from Skilled through Strategist. Others may use them with varying degrees of adeptness, independence or understanding, as illustrated by the performance expectations for each of the subsequent lower levels.

** Typically used by those from Expert through Strategist. Others may use them with varying degree of adeptness, independence or understanding, as illustrated by the performance expectations for each of the subsequent lower levels.

Requirements Analysis and Design Definition

7.1 Specify and Model Requirements

Definition

The purpose of Specify and Model Requirements is to analyze, synthesize, and refine elicitation results into requirements and designs.

Proficiency Descriptors

For descriptions on what each of the five levels mean, refer to the Proficiency Levels Legend.

5 - Strategist

- Continually monitor industry best practices in search of new ways to analyze, synthesize, and refine elicitation results into requirements and designs.

- Build templates and tools for enabling stakeholder-focused written communication, capturing the motivation, needs and requirements of stakeholders including:

  - stakeholder profiles, and

  - stakeholder-focused writing templates.

- Solicit and incorporate feedback from mentors/leaders as well as peers into performance improvement plans.

- Create innovative ways of performing this task using common techniques.

- Demonstrate Expert Proficiency Descriptors.

4 - Expert

- Apply business acumen when analyzing, synthesizing, and refining elicitation results into requirements and designs.

- Adopt approved approaches familiar to stakeholders.

- Have been:

  - recognized by colleagues as an authority at modelling requirements and designs, and

  - frequently engaged by peers for support.

- Lead and coach others on how to analyze, synthesize, and refine elicitation results into requirements and designs.

- Coach others on how to prepare and deliver written customer-focused communication.

- Guide others on how to effectively use common techniques.

- Demonstrate Skilled Proficiency Descriptors.

3 - Skilled

- Model requirements and designs.

- Analyze requirements and designs.

- Identify key information for requirements and designs, and their attributes.

- Develop the appropriate level of abstraction to meet the needs of the audience.

- Demonstrate an ability to learn quickly and willingly.

- Communicate complex concepts and data as understandable.

- Demonstrate well prepared, stakeholder-focused written communication.

- Invite stakeholder feedback and opinions to achieve understanding and agreement.

- Use common techniques.

2 - Practical Knowledge

- Can perform many of the tasks required to analyze, synthesize, and refine elicitation results into requirements and designs with support of others.

- Have a basic knowledge of, and can follow, instructions for common techniques.

1 - General Awareness

- Understand the importance of analyzing and refining elicitation results into requirements and designs.

- Have an awareness of common techniques.

Common Techniques

Table 7.1.1: Specify and Model Requirements - Common Techniques

Common Techniques	Usage
Acceptance and Evaluation Criteria	Used to represent the acceptance and evaluation criteria attributes of requirements.
Business Capability Analysis*	Used to represent features or functions of an enterprise.
Business Model Canvas*	Used to describe the rationale for requirements.
Business Rules Analysis	Used to analyze business rules so that they can be specified and modelled alongside requirements.
Concept Modelling	Used to define terms and relationships relevant to the change and the enterprise.
Data Dictionary	Used to record details about the data involved in the change. Details may include definitions, relationships with other data, origin, format, and usage.
Data Modelling	Used to model requirements to show how data will be used to meet stakeholder information needs.
Decision Modelling	Used to represent decisions in a model in order to show the elements of decision making required.
Functional Decomposition	Used to model requirements in order to identify constituent parts of an overall complex business function.
Glossary	Used to record the meaning of relevant business terms while analyzing requirements.
Interface Analysis	Used to model requirements in order to identify and validate inputs and outputs of the solution they are modelling.
Non-functional Requirements Analysis	Used to define and analyze the quality of service attributes.
Organizational Modelling	Used to allow business analysts to model the roles, responsibilities, and communications within an organization.

Table 7.1.1: Specify and Model Requirements - Common Techniques

Common Techniques	Usage
Process Modelling	Used to show the steps or activities that are performed in the organization, or that must be performed to meet the desired change.
Prototyping	Used to assist the stakeholders in visualizing the appearance and capabilities of a planned solution.
Roles and Permissions Matrix	Used to specify and model requirements concerned with the separation of duties among users and external interfaces in utilizing a solution.
Root Cause Analysis	Used to model the root causes of a problem as part of rationale.
Scope Modelling	Used to visually show a scope boundary.
Sequence Diagrams	Used to specify and model requirements to show how processes operate and interact with one another, and in what order.
Stakeholder Lists, Maps, or Personas	Used to identify the stakeholders and their characteristics.
State Modelling	Used to specify the different states of a part of the solution throughout a life cycle, in terms of the events that occur.
Use Cases and Scenarios	Used to model the desired behaviour of a solution, by showing user interactions with the solution, to achieve a specific goal or accomplish a particular task.
User Stories	Used to specify requirements as a brief statement about what people do or need to do when using the solution.

* Typically used by those from Expert through Strategist. Others may use them with varying degree of adeptness, independence or understanding, as illustrated by the performance expectations for each of the subsequent lower levels.

7.2   Verify Requirements

Definition

The purpose of Verify Requirements is to ensure that requirements and designs specifications and models meet quality standards and are usable for the purpose they serve.

Proficiency Descriptors

For descriptions on what each of the five levels mean, refer to the Proficiency Levels Legend.

5 - Strategist

- Continually monitor the industry in search of quality best practices to apply to requirements and designs specifications.

- · Develop and drive adoption of new methodologies as appropriate, and develop tools, templates, and processes to support those methodologies.

- Develop an innovative approach for using new tools, templates and processes that:

  - explain the rationale for adoption, and

  - invite intentional feedback and opinions from others.

- Capture requirements verification best practices and broadcast them to the business analysis community.

- Create new methods for identifying requirements verification criteria.

- Create innovative ways of performing this task using common techniques.

- Demonstrate Expert Proficiency Descriptors.

4 - Expert

- Meet regularly with peers and counterparts to discuss methods of ensuring design quality.

- Play multiple roles within activities prescribed by a methodology.

- Have been:

  - recognized by colleagues as an authority on quality of requirements and design specifications, and

  - frequently engaged by peers for quality support and advice.

- Coach others how to use the input from all stakeholders to make the most informed decisions.

- Guide others on how to effectively use common techniques.

- Demonstrate Skilled Proficiency Descriptors.

3 - Skilled

- Ensure the requirements meet the characteristics to support quality requirements and designs.

- Perform verification activities throughout the work.

- Use appropriate checklists for quality control.

- Demonstrate an understanding of the organization's nuances and how to get things done.

- Demonstrate capability in multiple analysis methodologies.

- Make and help others make the best decision based on appropriate criteria, such as business need, opportunities, risk, compliance and ability to achieve the desired outcome.

- Use common techniques.

2 - Practical Knowledge

- Understand which quality checklists to use.

- Can apply quality measures and practices developed by others.

- Have a basic knowledge of, and can follow, instructions for the common techniques.

1 - General Awareness

- Understand the importance of ensuring requirements and design specifications meet quality standards.

- Have an awareness of common techniques.

Common Techniques

Table 7.2.1: Verify Requirements - Common Techniques

Common Techniques	Usage
Acceptance and Evaluation Criteria	Used to ensure that requirements are stated clearly enough to devise a set of tests that can prove that the requirements have been met.
Item Tracking	Used to ensure that any problems or issues identified during verification are managed and resolved.

Table 7.2.1: Verify Requirements - Common Techniques (Continued)

Common Techniques	Usage
Metrics and Key Performance Indicators (KPIs)	Used to identify how to evaluate the quality of the requirements.
Reviews*	Used to inspect requirements documentation to identify requirements that are not of acceptable quality.

* Typically used by those from Skilled through Strategist. Others may use them with varying degrees of adeptness, independence or understanding, as illustrated by the performance expectations for each of the subsequent lower levels.

7.3 Validate Requirements

Definition

The purpose of Validate Requirements is to ensure that all requirements and designs align to the business requirements and support the delivery of needed value.

Proficiency Descriptors

For descriptions on what each of the five levels mean, refer to the Proficiency Levels Legend.

5 - Strategist

- Apply foresight when connecting concepts to enterprise components.

- Develop and drive adoption of new methodologies as appropriate, and develop tools, templates, and processes to support those methodologies.

- Develop an innovative approach for using new tools, templates and processes that:

  - explain the rationale for adoption, and

  - invite intentional feedback and opinions from others.

- Develop a network of Subject Matter Experts (SMEs) inside and outside of the organization in order to:

  - contribute knowledge/skill into the network, and

  - draw knowledge/skill from the network appropriately.

- Have been:

  - recognized by leadership as an authority in aligning requirements and designs to business requirements, and

  - frequently assigned complex projects.

- Create innovative ways of performing this task using common techniques.

- Demonstrate Expert Proficiency Descriptors.

4 - Expert

- Clearly communicate concepts to relevant stakeholders, and follow up to verify their understanding and approval.

- Develop a network of SMEs within the organization.

- Have been recognized as an authority in several analysis methodologies, and as a result:

  - have been asked by leadership to spearhead change in methodologies, and

  - have been asked by peers for advice and support.

- Have been:

  - recognized by colleagues as an authority in aligning requirements and designs to business requirements, and

  - frequently engaged by peers for quality support and advice.

- Maintain and continuously enhance communications channels with stakeholders to ensure that issues surface and are managed in a timely fashion.

- Guide others on how to effectively use common techniques.

- Demonstrate Skilled Proficiency Descriptors.

3 - Skilled

- Identify assumptions and utilize them to manage risks.

- Define measurable evaluation criteria to assess the success of the change.

- Evaluate alignment with solution scope to support value delivery.

- Demonstrate an understanding of the organization's nuances and how to get things done.

- Demonstrate capability in multiple analysis methodologies.

- Analyze and use a holistic view of people, processes and technology to understand the enterprise.

- Use common techniques.

2 - Practical Awareness

- Can align requirements/designs and business requirements with support from others.

- Have a basic knowledge of, and can follow, instructions for common techniques.

1 - General Knowledge

- Understand the importance of ensuring requirements and designs support delivery of value.

- Understand the business requirements that the designs are intended to address.

- Have an awareness of common techniques.

Common Techniques

Table 7.3.1: Validate Requirements - Common Techniques

Common Techniques	Usage
Acceptance and Evaluation Criteria	Used to define the quality metrics that must be met to achieve acceptance by a stakeholder.
Document Analysis	Used to identify previously documented business needs in order to validate requirements.
Financial Analysis*	Used to define the financial benefits associated with requirements.
Item Tracking	Used to ensure that any problems or issues identified during validation are managed and resolved.
Metrics and Key Performance Indicators (KPIs)	Used to select appropriate performance measures for a solution, solution component, or requirement.
Reviews*	Used to confirm whether or not the stakeholder agrees that their needs are met.
Risk Analysis & Management*	Used to identify possible scenarios that would alter the benefit delivered by a requirement.

* Typically used by those from Skilled through Strategist. Others may use them with varying degrees of adeptness, independence or understanding, as illustrated by the performance expectations for each of the subsequent lower levels.

7.4   Define Requirements Architecture

Definition

The purpose of Define Requirements Architecture is to ensure that the requirements collectively support one another to fully achieve the objectives.

Proficiency Descriptors

For descriptions on what each of the five levels mean, refer to the Proficiency Levels Legend.

5 - Strategist

- Develop and drive adoption of frameworks to develop the requirements architecture.

- Develop new and innovative approaches to requirements architecture.

- Develop and drive adoption of new methodologies as appropriate, and develop tools, templates, and processes to support those methodologies.

- Develop an innovative approach for using new tools, templates and processes that:

    - explain the rationale for adoption, and

    - invite intentional feedback and opinions from others.

- Have been frequently sought out by stakeholders for critical thinking/ analytical/problem solving ability.

- Create innovative ways of performing this task using common techniques.

- Demonstrate Expert Proficiency Descriptors.

4 - Expert

- Consistently ensure complex requirements support one another.

- Regularly solicit requirement viewpoints from relevant stakeholders.

- Play multiple roles within activities prescribed by a methodology.

- Convert complex ideas into easy concepts.

- Have been:

    - recognized by colleagues as an authority in developing requirements architecture, and,

    - frequently engaged by peers for support.

- Coach others on how to ensure requirements support one another.

- Guide others on how to effectively use common techniques.

- Demonstrate Skilled Proficiency Descriptors.

3 - Skilled

- Make effective use of requirement viewpoints and views.

- Leverage templates to develop the requirements architecture.

- Ensure that:
  - the set of requirements is complete; it is cohesive and tells the audience the full story, and
  - the requirements relate to each other by identifying requirement relationships.

- Define the business analysis information architecture.

- Demonstrate capability in multiple analysis methodologies.

- Use a structured approach to problem solving.

- Put all the pieces together to ensure that the requirements collectively support one another to fully achieve the objectives.

- Use common techniques.

2 - Practical Awareness

- Can ensure basic requirements support one another, with support from others.

- Have a basic knowledge of, and can follow, instructions for common techniques.

1 - General Knowledge

- Understand the importance of ensuring requirements support one another.

- Have an awareness of common techniques.

Common Techniques

Table 7.4.1: Define Requirements Architecture - Common Techniques

Common Techniques	Usage
Data Modelling	Used to describe the requirements structure as it relates to data.
Functional Decomposition	Used to break down an organizational unit, product scope, or other elements into its component parts.
Interviews	Used to define the requirements structure collaboratively.

Table 7.4.1: Define Requirements Architecture - Common Techniques

Common Techniques	Usage
Organizational Modelling	Used to understand the various organizational units, stakeholders, and their relationships which might help define relevant viewpoints.
Scope Modelling	Used to identify the elements and boundaries of the requirements architecture.
Workshops	Used to define the requirements structure collaboratively.

7.5   Define Design Options

Definition

The purpose of Define Design Options is to define the solution approach, identify business improvement opportunities, allocate requirements across solution components, and develop design options that achieve the desired future state.

Proficiency Descriptors

For descriptions on what each of the five levels mean, refer to the Proficiency Levels Legend.

5 - Strategist

- Continually monitor the industry in search of best practices that lead to more effective design options.

- Apply foresight when connecting concepts to enterprise components.

- Develop a network of Subject Matter Experts (SMEs) inside and outside of the organization in order to:

    - contribute knowledge/skill into the network, and

    - draw knowledge/skill from the network appropriately.

- Have been:

    - recognized by leadership as an authority in developing design options that achieved the desired future state, and

    - frequently assigned high visibility and/or complex projects.

- Create innovative ways of performing this task using common techniques.

- Demonstrate Expert Proficiency Descriptors.

4 - Expert

- Consistently develop effective designs with complex requirements.
- Apply insight and business acumen when connecting concepts as they relate to different aspects of the enterprise.
- Develop a network of SMEs within the organization.
- Have been:
  - recognized by colleagues as an authority in developing design options that achieved the desired future state, and
  - frequently engaged by peers for support.
- Guide others on how to effectively use common techniques.
- Demonstrate Skilled Proficiency Descriptors.

3 - Skilled

- Identify appropriate solution approaches.
- Identify improvement opportunities.
- Allocate requirements to solution components and releases to best achieve change objectives.
- Develop design options aligned with the desired future state.
- Demonstrate an understanding of the organization's nuances and how to get things done.
- Analyze and use a holistic view of people, processes and technology to understand the enterprise.
- Put all the pieces together to define the solution approach, identify business improvement opportunities, allocate requirements across solution components, and develop design options that achieve the desired future state.
- Use common techniques.

2 - Practical Awareness

- Can develop design options with basic requirements, with support from others.
- Have a basic knowledge of, and can follow, instructions for common techniques.

1 - General Knowledge

- Understand the importance of developing design options that achieve the desired future state.
- Have an awareness of common techniques.

Common Techniques

Table 7.5.1: Define Design Options - Common Techniques

Common Techniques	Usage
Benchmarking & Market Analysis**	Used to identify and analyze existing solutions and market trends.
Brainstorming	Used to help identify improvement opportunities and design options.
Document Analysis	Used to provide information needed to describe design options and design elements.
Interviews	Used to help identify improvement opportunities and design options.
Lessons Learned	Used to help identify improvement opportunities.
Mind Mapping*	Used to identify and explore possible design options.
Root Cause Analysis	Used to understand the underlying cause of the problems being addressed in the change to propose solutions to address them.
Survey or Questionnaire	Used to help identify improvement opportunities and design options.
Vendor Assessment**	Used to couple the assessment of a third party solution with an assessment of the vendor to ensure that the solution is viable and all parties will be able to develop and maintain a healthy working relationship.
Workshops	Used to help identify improvement opportunities and design options.

* Typically used by those from Skilled through Strategist. Others may use them with varying degrees of adeptness, independence or understanding, as illustrated by the performance expectations for each of the subsequent lower levels.

** Typically used by those from Expert through Strategist. Others may use them with varying degree of adeptness, independence or understanding, as illustrated by the performance expectations for each of the subsequent lower levels.

7.6   Analyze Potential Value and Recommend Solution

Definition

The purpose of Analyze Potential Value and Recommend Solution is to determine which design option best meets requirements after analyzing the potential value for each option.

Proficiency Descriptors

For descriptions on what each of the five levels mean, refer to the Proficiency Levels Legend.

5 - Strategist

- Develop approaches and tactics for developing greater organizational understanding.

- Create new methods for locating data and how to analyze its accuracy and importance in determining potential value.

- Capture best practices in analyzing potential value and solution recommendation and broadcast them to the business analysis community.

- Have been:

  - recognized by stakeholders as an authority in identifying the highest value alternatives, and

  - typically successful in having stakeholders follow recommendations.

- Create innovative ways of performing this task using common techniques.

- Demonstrate Expert Proficiency Descriptors.

4 - Expert

- Consistently articulate complex design options in simple terms, so the audience understands its value.

- Consistently synthesize complex data from disparate sources and understand how they impact the enterprise or organization.

- Bring stakeholders together and consider differing viewpoints when analyzing potential value.

- Have been frequently engaged by peers for advice and support on analyzing potential value and recommending solutions.

- Coach others how to use the input from all stakeholders to make the most informed decisions.

- Guide others on how to effectively use common techniques.

- Demonstrate Skilled Proficiency Descriptors.

3 - Skilled

- Identify:
  - the benefits that a potential solution is expected to deliver, and
  - the costs associated with a potential solution.
- Determine the value of a solution to key stakeholders.
- Assess design options and recommend the appropriate solution.
- Demonstrate an understanding of the organization's nuances and how to get things done.
- Analyze and use a holistic view of people, processes and technology to understand the enterprise.
- Make and help others make the best decision based on appropriate criteria, such as:
  - business need,
  - opportunities,
  - risk,
  - compliance, and
  - the ability to achieve the desired outcome.
- Leverage an understanding of the organization to identify the most effective means of implementing a change.
- Use common techniques.

2 - Practical Awareness

- Can perform some, but not all, of the tasks required to analyze design options, with support from others.
- Have a basic knowledge of, and can follow, instructions for common techniques.

1 - General Knowledge

- Understand the importance of analyzing design options and making an appropriate recommendation.
- Have an awareness of common techniques.

Common Techniques

Table 7.6.1: Analyze Potential Value and Recommend Solution- Common Techniques

Common Techniques	Usage
Acceptance and Evaluation Criteria	Used to express requirements in the form of acceptance criteria to make them most useful when assessing proposed solutions and determining whether a solution meets the defined business needs.
Backlog Management	Used to sequence the potential value.
Brainstorming	Used to identify potential benefits of the requirements in a collaborative manner.
Business Cases*	Used to assess recommendations against business goals and objectives.
Business Model Canvas**	Used as a tool to help understand strategy and initiatives.
Decision Analysis	Used to support the assessment and ranking of design options.
Estimation	Used to forecast the costs and efforts of meeting the requirements as a step towards estimating their value.
Financial Analysis	Used to evaluate the financial return of different options and choose the best possible return on investment.
Focus Groups	Used to get stakeholder input on which design options best meet the requirements, and to evaluate a targeted, small group of stakeholders' value expectations.
Interviews	Used to get stakeholder input on which design options best meet the requirements, and to evaluate individual stakeholders' value expectations.
Metrics and Key Performance Indicators (KPIs)	Used to create and evaluate the measurements used in defining value.
Risk Analysis & Management*	Used to identify and manage the risks that could affect the potential value of the requirements.

Table 7.6.1: Analyze Potential Value and Recommend Solution- Common Techniques (Continued)

Common Techniques	Usage
Survey or Questionnaire	Used to get stakeholder input on which design options best meet the requirements, and to identify stakeholders' value expectations.
SWOT Analysis	Used to identify areas of strength and weakness that will impact the value of the solutions.
Workshops	Used to get stakeholder input on which design options best meet the requirements, and to evaluate stakeholders' value expectations.

* Typically used by those from Skilled through Strategist. Others may use them with varying degrees of adeptness, independence or understanding, as illustrated by the performance expectations for each of the subsequent lower levels.

** Typically used by those from Expert through Strategist. Others may use them with varying degree of adeptness, independence or understanding, as illustrated by the performance expectations for each of the subsequent lower levels.

8 Solution Evaluation

8.1 Measure Solution Performance

Definition

The purpose of Measure Solution Performance is to define performance measures and assess the data collected to evaluate solution effectiveness.

Proficiency Descriptors

For descriptions on what each of the five levels mean, refer to the Proficiency Levels Legend.

5 - Strategist

- Develop new and innovative evaluation method(s), including metrics, measurement tools, etc.
- Develop an innovative approach for using new tools, templates and processes that:
    - explain the rationale for adoption, and
    - invite intentional feedback and opinions from others.
- Document rules and best practices for when to use which method of communication.
- Capture best practices in measuring solution performance and broadcast them to the business analysis community.
- Create innovative ways of performing this task using common techniques.
- Demonstrate Expert Proficiency Descriptors.

4 - Expert

- Take existing evaluation methods and apply them in new ways to address solution evaluation.

- Consistently uncover emotional drivers of stakeholders and develop messaging accordingly.

- Have been:

    - recognized as an authority in several analysis methodologies, and

    - asked by leadership to spearhead change in methodologies.

- Have been frequently engaged by peers for advice and support.

- Guide others on how to effectively use common techniques.

- Demonstrate Skilled Proficiency Descriptors.

3 - Skilled

- Identify the appropriate measures to use to assess solution performance.

- Validate the performance measures selected with key stakeholders.

- Independently assess appropriate performance measures that can be used to assess solution performance.

- Demonstrate an understanding of the organization's nuances and how to get things done.

- Demonstrate capability in multiple analysis methodologies.

- Leverage an understanding of the organization to identify the most effective means of implementing a change.

- Demonstrate proficiency in using office applications to document, track and communicate performance measures and the data collected to evaluate solution effectiveness.

- Adapt verbal and non-verbal communication style to the needs of the situation and the individual.

- Use common techniques.

2 - Practical Knowledge

- Measure solution effectiveness using criteria defined by others.

- Define performance measures and assess collected data with support from others.

- Have a basic knowledge of and able to follow instructions for common techniques.

1 - General Awareness

- Understand the importance of evaluating solution effectiveness.

- Have an awareness of common techniques.

Common Techniques

Table 8.1.1: Measure Solution Performance - Common Techniques

Common Techniques	Usage
Acceptance and Evaluations Criteria	Used to define acceptable solution performance.
Benchmarking & Market Analysis**	Used to define measures and their acceptable levels.
Business Cases*	Used to define business objectives and performance measures for a proposed solution.
Data Mining	Used to collect and analyze large amounts of data regarding solution performance.
Decision Analysis	Used to assist stakeholders in deciding on suitable ways to measure solution performance and acceptable levels of performance.
Focus Groups	Used to provide subjective assessments, insights, and impressions of a solution's performance.
Metrics and Key Performance Indicators (KPIs)	Used to measure solution performance.
Non-functional Requirements Analysis	Used to define expected characteristics of a solution.
Observation	Used either to provide feedback on perceptions of solution performance or to reconcile contradictory results.
Prototyping	Used to simulate a new solution so that performance measures can be determined and collected.
Survey or Questionnaire	Used to gather opinions and attitudes about solution performance. Surveys and questionnaires can be effective when large or disparate groups need to be polled.

Table 8.1.1: Measure Solution Performance - Common Techniques

Common Techniques	Usage
Use Cases and Scenarios	Used to define the expected outcomes of a solution.
Vendor Assessment**	Used to assess which of the vendor's performance measures should be included in the solution's performance assessment.

* Typically used by those from Skilled through Strategist. Others may use them with varying degrees of adeptness, independence or understanding, as illustrated by the performance expectations for each of the subsequent lower levels.

** Typically used by those from Expert through Strategist. Others may use them with varying degree of adeptness, independence or understanding, as illustrated by the performance expectations for each of the subsequent lower levels.

8.2   Analyze Performance Measures

Definition

The purpose of Analyze Performance Measures is to provide insights into solution performance based on the value it delivers.

Proficiency Descriptors

For descriptions on what each of the five levels mean, refer to the Proficiency Levels Legend.

5 - Strategist

- Apply foresight to predict and avoid risk.
- Apply foresight when connecting concepts to enterprise components.
- Develop and drive adoption of tools, templates, and processes for measuring and analyzing solution performance.
- Develop an innovative approach for using new tools, templates and processes that:
  - explain the rationale for adoption, and
  - invite intentional feedback and opinions from others.
- Analyze business related metrics found on documents such as financial statements and make appropriate recommendations.
- Develop nontraditional ideas for analyzing performance measures.
- Create innovative ways of performing this task using common techniques.
- Demonstrate Expert Proficiency Descriptors.

4 - Expert

- Monitor historical data to identify systemic issues and best practices.

- Apply insight and business acumen when connecting concepts as they relate to different aspects of the enterprise.

- Focus learning on using business acumen.

- Help others understand the solution's impact on business related metrics such as operating costs, revenues and customer profit margins.

- Guide others on how to effectively use common techniques.

- Demonstrate Skilled Proficiency Descriptors.

3 - Skilled

- Examine the performance measures collected to assess solution performance against the desired value.

- Highlight risks identified through assessing the performance measures.

- Assess performance measures to identify relevant trends.

- Test and analyze performance measures to ensure their accuracy.

- Identify performance variances, their root cause, and recommend appropriate actions to reduce variance.

- Demonstrate the ability to incorporate business and industry knowledge into work.

- Analyze and use a holistic view of people, processes and technology to understand the enterprise.

- Demonstrate an ability to learn quickly and willingly to apply insights into solution performance based on the value it delivers.

- Use common techniques.

2 - Practical Knowledge

- Occasionally test and analyze performance measures to ensure accuracy.

- Have a basic knowledge of and able to follow instructions for common techniques.

1 - General Awareness

- Understand the need to analyze performance measures.

- Rely on others to provide insight into solution performance.

- Have an awareness of common techniques.

Common Techniques

Table 8.2.1: Analyze Performance Measures - Common Techniques

Common Techniques	Usage
Acceptance and Evaluations Criteria	Used to define acceptable solution performance through acceptance criteria. The degree of variance from these criteria will guide the analysis of that performance.
Benchmarking & Market Analysis**	Used to observe the results of other organizations employing similar solutions when assessing risks, trends, and variances.
Data Mining	Used to collect data regarding performance, trends, common issues, and variances from expected performance levels and understand patterns and meaning in that data.
Interviews	Used to determine expected value of a solution and its perceived performance from an individual or small group's perspective.
Metrics and Key Performance Indicators (KPIs)	Used to analyze solution performance, especially when judging how well a solution contributes to achieving goals.
Observation	Used to observe a solution in action if the data collected does not provide definitive conclusions.
Risk Analysis & Management*	Used to identify, analyze, develop plans to modify the risks, and to manage the risks on an ongoing basis.
Root Cause Analysis	Used to determine the underlying cause of performance variance.
Survey or Questionnaire	Used to determine expected value of a solution and its perceived performance.

* Typically used by those from Skilled through Strategist. Others may use them with varying degrees of adeptness, independence or understanding, as illustrated by the performance expectations for each of the subsequent lower levels.

** Typically used by those from Expert through Strategist. Others may use them with varying degree of adeptness, independence or understanding, as illustrated by the performance expectations for each of the subsequent lower levels.

8.3   Assess Solution Limitations

Definition

The purpose of Assess Solution Limitations is to determine factors internal to the solution that restrict the full realization of value.

Proficiency Descriptors

For descriptions on what each of the five levels mean, refer to the Proficiency Levels Legend.

5 - Strategist

- Create and drive adoption of tools, templates, and processes that help identify the internal factors that restrict full realization of the solution's value.

- Develop new and innovative methodologies for problem solving and critical thinking.

- Develop an innovative approach for using new tools, templates and processes that:

  - explain the rationale for adoption, and

  - invite intentional feedback and opinions from others.

- Develop nontraditional ideas for assessing solution limitations.

- Capture best practices on assessing solution limitations and broadcast them to the business analysis community.

- Have been:

  - recognized by leadership as an authority in understanding complex relationships at an enterprise level, and

  - frequently assigned to high visibility and high risk initiatives.

- Create innovative ways of performing this task using common techniques.

- Demonstrate Expert Proficiency Descriptors.

4 - Expert

- Propose the following:

  - alternative solutions to problems or opportunities, and

  - informed recommendations based on evaluation of the solutions' merits.

- Consistently identify opportunities to contribute to the solution's value.

- Utilize proven methodologies for problem solving and critical thinking.

- Consistently synthesize complex data from disparate sources and understand how they impact the enterprise or organization.

- Apply business acumen when exploring the root cause for under-performing and ineffective solutions and components.

- Have been:

    - recognized by colleagues as an authority in determining the internal factors that restrict full realization of the solution's value, and

    - frequently engaged by peers for support.

- Guide others on how to effectively use common techniques.

- Demonstrate Skilled Proficiency Descriptors.

3 - Skilled

- Identify internal solution component dependencies.

- Perform problem analysis to identify the source of solution limitations.

- Perform impact assessment activities to quantify factors that affect solution performance

- Analyze and use a holistic view of people, processes and technology to understand the enterprise in order to:

    - identify and validate assumptions to highlight solution limitations, and

    - identify risks and mitigation measures when leveraging the holistic view.

- Use a structured approach to problem solving.

- Collect stakeholder feedback and agreement on an approach to identify and resolve problems.

- Demonstrate an ability to learn quickly and willingly about factors internal to the solution that restrict full realization of value.

- Demonstrate an understanding of the organization's nuances and how to get things done.

- Demonstrate the ability to incorporate business and industry knowledge into work.

- Use common techniques.

2 - Practical Knowledge

- Can determine the internal factors that restrict full realization of the solution's value with support of others.

- Leverage best practices developed by others.

- Have a basic knowledge of and able to follow instructions for common techniques.

1 - General Awareness

- Understand the importance of determining the internal factors that restrict full realization of the solution's value.

- Have an awareness of common techniques.

Common Techniques

Table 8.3.1: Assess Solution Limitations - Common Techniques

Common Techniques	Usage
Acceptance and Evaluation Criteria	Used both to indicate the level at which acceptance criteria are met or anticipated to be met by the solution and to identify any criteria that are not met by the solution.
Benchmarking & Market Analysis**	Used to assess if other organizations are experiencing the same solution challenges and, if possible, determine how they are addressing it.
Business Rules Analysis	Used to illustrate the current business rules and the changes required to achieve the potential value of the change.
Data Mining	Used to identify factors constraining performance of the solution.
Decision Analysis	Used to illustrate the current business decisions and the changes required to achieve the potential value of the change.
Interviews	Used to help perform problem analysis.
Item Tracking	Used to record and manage stakeholder issues related to why the solution is not meeting the potential value.
Lessons Learned	Used to determine what can be learned from the inception, definition, and construction of the solution to have potentially impacted its ability to deliver value.
Risk Analysis & Management*	Used to identify, analyze, and manage risks, as they relate to the solution and its potential limitations, that may impede the realization of potential value.
Root Cause Analysis	Used to identify and understand the combination of factors and their underlying causes that led to the solution being unable to deliver its potential value.
Survey or Questionnaire	Used to help perform problem analysis.

* Typically used by those from Skilled through Strategist. Others may use them with varying degrees of adeptness, independence or understanding, as illustrated by the performance expectations for each of the subsequent lower levels.

** Typically used by those from Expert through Strategist. Others may use them with varying degree of adeptness, independence or understanding, as illustrated by the performance expectations for each of the subsequent lower levels.

8.4 Assess Enterprise Limitations

Definition

The purpose of Assess Enterprise Limitations is to determine how factors external to the solution are restricting full realization of value.

Proficiency Descriptors

For descriptions on what each of the five levels mean, refer to the Proficiency Levels Legend.

5 - Strategist

- Monitor the industry in search of approaches or insights to determine and overcome the external factors that restrict the solution's full realization of value.

- Create and drive adoption of tools, templates, and processes that help identify the external factors that restrict full realization of the solution's value.

- Develop an innovative approach for using new tools, templates and processes that:

  - explain the rationale for adoption, and

  - invite intentional feedback and opinions from others.

- Apply foresight when connecting concepts to enterprise components.

- Consistently identify the root cause of systemic issues.

- Develop nontraditional ideas for assessing enterprise limitations.

- Develop a network of Subject Matter Experts (SMEs) inside and outside of the organization and do the following:

  - contribute knowledge/skill into the network, and

  - draw knowledge/skill from the network appropriately.

- Create innovative ways of performing this task using common techniques.

- Demonstrate Expert Proficiency Descriptors.

4 - Expert

- Consistently identify opportunities to contribute to the solution's value.

- Consistently synthesize complex data from disparate sources and understand how they impact the enterprise or organization.

- Leverage historical data to resolve current challenges.

- Receptive to nontraditional ways of learning ideas.

- Develop a network of SMEs within the organization.

- Have been:

  - recognized by colleagues as an authority in determining the internal factors that restrict full realization of the solution's value, and

  - frequently engaged by peers for support.

- Guide others on how to effectively use common techniques.

- Demonstrate Skilled Proficiency Descriptors.

3 - Skilled

- Assess enterprise culture.

- Complete stakeholder impact analysis.

- Assess how a solution impacts the organizational structure.

- Perform an operational assessment on processes and technology.

- Demonstrate an understanding of the organization's nuances and how to get things done.

- Analyze and use a holistic view of people, processes and technology to understand the enterprise.

- Sees stakeholder feedback and consensus to identify constraints and devise alternatives.

- Use a structured approach to problem solving.

- Demonstrate an ability to learn quickly and willingly about factors external to the solution that restrict full realization of value.

- Demonstrate the ability to incorporate business and industry knowledge into work.

- Use common techniques.

2 - Practical Knowledge

- Can determine the external factors that restrict full realization of the solution's value with support of others.

- Leverage best practices developed by others.

- Have a basic knowledge of and able to follow instructions for common techniques.

1 - General Awareness

- Understand the importance of determining the external factors that restrict full realization of the solution's value.

- Have an awareness of common techniques.

Common Techniques

Table 8.4.1: Assess Enterprise Limitations - Common Techniques

Common Techniques	Usage
Benchmarking & Market Analysis**	Used to identify existing solutions and enterprise interactions.
Brainstorming	Used to identify organizational gaps or stakeholder concerns.
Data Mining	Used to identify factors constraining performance of the solution.
Decision Analysis	Used to assist in making an optimal decision under conditions of uncertainty and may be used in the assessment to make decisions about functional, technical, or procedural gaps.
Document Analysis	Used to gain an understanding of the culture, operations, and structure of the organization.
Interviews	Used to identify organizational gaps or stakeholder concerns.
Item Tracking	Used to ensure that issues are not neglected or lost and that issues identified by assessment are resolved.
Lessons Learned	Used to analyze previous initiatives and the enterprise interactions with the solutions.
Observation	Used to witness the enterprise and solution interactions to identify impacts.
Organizational Modelling	Used to ensure the identification of any required changes to the organizational structure that may have to be addressed.
Process Analysis	Used to identify possible opportunities to improve performance.

Table 8.4.1: Assess Enterprise Limitations - Common Techniques

Common Techniques	Usage
Process Modelling	Used to illustrate the current business processes and/or changes that must be made in order to achieve the potential value of the solution.
Risk Analysis & Management*	Used to consider risk in the areas of technology (if the selected technological resources provide required functionality), finance (if costs could exceed levels that make the change salvageable), and business (if the organization will be able to make the changes necessary to attain potential value from the solution).
Roles and Permissions Matrix	Used to determine roles and associated permissions for stakeholders, as well as stability of end users.
Root Cause Analysis	Used to determine if the underlying cause may be related to enterprise limitations.
Survey or Questionnaire	Used to identify organizational gaps or stakeholder concerns.
SWOT Analysis	Used to demonstrate how a change will help the organization maximize strengths and minimize weaknesses, and to assess strategies developed to respond to identified issues.
Workshops	Used to identify organizational gaps or stakeholder concerns.

* Typically used by those from Skilled through Strategist. Others may use them with varying degrees of adeptness, independence or understanding, as illustrated by the performance expectations for each of the subsequent lower levels.

** Typically used by those from Expert through Strategist. Others may use them with varying degree of adeptness, independence or understanding, as illustrated by the performance expectations for each of the subsequent lower levels.

8.5 Recommend Actions to Increase Solution Value

Definition

The purpose of Recommend Actions to Increase Solution Value is to determine how factors external to the solution are restricting full realization of value.

Proficiency Descriptors

For descriptions on what each of the five levels mean, refer to the Proficiency Levels Legend.

5 - Strategist

- Create new ways to assess the possibilities of a situation.

- Develop approaches and tactics for developing greater organizational understanding.

- Develop a network of Subject Matter Experts (SMEs) inside and outside of the organization and do the following:

  - contribute knowledge/skill into the network, and

  - draw knowledge/skill from the network appropriately.

- Have been:

  - recognized by leadership as an authority in recommending actions that maximize value,

  - frequently asked for input, and

  - asked for recommendations are typically implemented by leadership.

- Create innovative ways of performing this task using common techniques.

- Demonstrate Expert Proficiency Descriptors.

4 - Expert

- Consistently identify opportunities to contribute to the solution's value.

- Clearly communicate concepts to relevant stakeholders, and follow up to verify their understanding and approval.

- Develop a network of SMEs within the organization.

- Coach others how to use the input from all stakeholders to make the most informed decisions.

- Guide others on how to effectively use common techniques.

- Demonstrate Skilled Proficiency Descriptors.

3 - Skilled

- Ensure appropriate solution performance measures are being used.

- Provide substantiated recommendations.

- Collect stakeholder feedback and consensus on recommended approaches.

- Demonstrate an understanding of the organization's nuances and how to get things done.

- Analyze and use a holistic view of people, processes and technology to understand the enterprise

- Make and help others make the best decision based on appropriate criteria, such as:

  - business need,

  - opportunities,

  - risk,

  - compliance, and

  - the ability to achieve the desired outcome.

- Use common techniques.

2 - Practical Knowledge

- Can recommend basic actions to align the factors that create the difference between potential value and actual value with the support of others.

- Leverage best practices developed by others.

- Have a basic knowledge of and able to follow instructions for common techniques.

1 - General Awareness

- Understand the importance of recommending actions to align the factors that create the difference between potential value and actual value.

- Have an awareness of common techniques.

Common Techniques

Table 8.5.1: Recommend Actions to Increase Solution Value - Common Techniques

Common Techniques	Usage
Data Mining	Used to generate predictive estimates of solution performance.
Decision Analysis*	Used to determine the impact of acting on any of the potential value or performance issues.
Financial Analysis*	Used to assess the potential costs and benefits of a change.
Focus Groups	Used to determine if solution performance measures need to be adjusted and used to identify potential opportunities to improve performance.
Organizational Modelling	Used to demonstrate potential change within the organization's structure.

Table 8.5.1: Recommend Actions to Increase Solution Value - Common Techniques (Continued)

Common Techniques	Usage
Prioritization	Used to identify relative value of different actions to improve solution performance.
Process Analysis	Used to identify opportunities within related processes.
Risk Analysis & Management	Used to evaluate different outcomes under specific conditions.
Survey or Questionnaire	Used to gather feedback from a wide variety of stakeholders to determine if value has been met or exceeded, if the metrics are still valid or relevant in the current context, and what actions might be taken to improve the solution.

* Typically used by those from Skilled through Strategist. Others may use them with varying degrees of adeptness, independence or understanding, as illustrated by the performance expectations for each of the subsequent lower levels

Appendix A: Underlying Competencies

The Underlying Competencies chapter provides a description of the behaviours, characteristics, knowledge, and personal qualities that support the practice of business analysis.

The underlying competencies described here are not unique to business analysis. They are described here to ensure readers are aware of the range of fundamental skills required and provide a basis for them to further investigate the skills and knowledge that will enable them to be accomplished and adaptable business analysts.

These competencies are grouped into six categories:

- Analytical Thinking and Problem Solving,
- Behavioural Characteristics,
- Business Knowledge,
- Communication Skills,
- Interaction Skills, and
- Tools and Technology.

Each underlying competency is defined with a purpose, definition, and effectiveness measures.

A.1   Analytical Thinking and Problem Solving

Analytical thinking and problem solving skills are required for business analysts to analyze problems and opportunities effectively, identify which changes may deliver the most value, and work with stakeholders to understand the impact of those changes.

Business analysts use analytical thinking by rapidly assimilating various types of information (for example, diagrams, stakeholder concerns, customer feedback, schematics, user guides, and spreadsheets), and identifying which are relevant. Business analysts should be able to quickly choose effective and adaptable methods to learn and analyze the media, audiences, problem types, and environments as each is encountered.

Business analysts utilize analytical thinking and problem solving as they facilitate understanding of situations, the value of proposed changes, and other complex ideas.

Possessing a sound understanding of the analytical thinking and problem solving core competencies allows business analysts to identify the best ways to present information to their stakeholders. For example, some concepts are more easily understood when presented in diagrams and information graphics rather than by paragraphs of text. Having this understanding assists business analysts when planning their business analysis approach and enables them to communicate business analysis information in a manner that suits the material being conveyed to their audience.

Analytical Thinking and Problem Solving core competencies include:

- Creative Thinking,
- Decision Making,
- Learning,
- Problem Solving,
- Systems Thinking,
- Conceptual Thinking, and
- Visual Thinking.

Creative Thinking

Purpose

Thinking creatively and helping others to apply creative thinking helps business analysts to be effective in generating new ideas, approaches, and alternatives to problem solving and opportunities.

Definition

Creative thinking involves generating new ideas and concepts as well as finding new or different associations between existing ideas and concepts. It helps overcome rigid approaches to problem solving by questioning conventional approaches and encouraging new ideas and innovations that are appropriate to the situation. Creative thinking may involve combining, changing, and reapplying existing concepts or ideas. Business analysts can be effective in promoting creative thinking in others by identifying and proposing alternatives, and by asking questions and challenging assumptions.

Effectiveness Measures

Measures of effective creative thinking include:

- generating and productively considering new ideas,
- exploring concepts and ideas that are new,
- exploring changes to existing concepts and ideas,
- generating creativity for self and others, and
- applying new ideas to resolve existing problems.

Decision Making

Purpose

Business analysts must be effective in understanding the criteria involved in making a decision, and in assisting others to make better decisions.

Definition

When a business analyst or a group of stakeholders is faced with having to select an option from a set of alternatives, a decision must be made on which is the most advantageous for the stakeholders and the enterprise. Determining this involves gathering the information that is relevant to the decision, analyzing the relevant information, making comparisons and trade-offs between similar and dissimilar options, and identifying the most desirable option. Business analysts document decisions (and the rationale supporting those decisions) to use them as a reference in the event a similar decision is required in the future or if they are required to explain why a decision was made.

Effectiveness Measures

Measures of effective decision making include:

- the appropriate stakeholders are represented in the decision-making process,
- stakeholders understand the decision-making process and the rationale behind the decision,
- the pros and cons of all available options are clearly communicated to stakeholders,
- the decision reduces or eliminates uncertainty, and any remaining uncertainty is accepted,
- the decision made addresses the need or the opportunity at hand and is in the best interest of all stakeholders,
- stakeholders understand all the conditions, environment, and measures in which the decision will be made, and
- a decision is made.

Learning

Purpose

The ability to quickly absorb new and different types of information and also modify and adapt existing knowledge allows business analysts to work effectively in rapidly changing and evolving environments.

Definition

Learning is the process of gaining knowledge or skills. Learning about a domain passes through a set of stages, from initial acquisition and learning of raw facts, through comprehension of their meaning, to applying the knowledge in day-to-day work, and finally analysis, synthesis, and evaluation. Business analysts must be able to describe their level of understanding of the business domain and be capable of applying that level of understanding to determine which analysis activities need to be performed in a given situation. Once learning about a domain has reached the point where analysis is complete, business analysts must be able to synthesize the information to identify opportunities to create new solutions and evaluate those solutions to ensure that they are effective.

Learning is improved when the learning technique is selected based on the required learning outcomes.

Learning techniques to consider include:

- Visual: learning through the presentation of pictures, photographs, diagrams, models, and videos.

- Auditory: learning through verbal and written language and text.

- Kinesthetic: learning by doing.

Most people experience faster understanding and longer retention of information when more than one learning technique is used.

Effectiveness Measures

Measures of effective learning include:

- understanding that learning is a process for all stakeholders,

- learning the concepts presented and then demonstrating an understanding of them,

- demonstrating the ability to apply concepts to new areas or relationships,

- rapidly absorbing new facts, ideas, concepts, and opinions, and

- effectively presenting new facts, ideas, concepts, and opinions to others.

Problem Solving

Purpose

Business analysts define and solve problems in order to ensure that the real, underlying root cause of a problem is understood by all stakeholders and that solution options address that root cause.

Definition

Defining a problem involves ensuring that the nature of the problem and any underlying issues are clearly understood by all stakeholders. Stakeholder points of view are articulated and addressed to understand any conflicts between the goals and objectives of different groups of stakeholders. Assumptions are identified and validated. The objectives that will be met once the problem is solved are clearly specified, and alternative solutions are considered and possibly developed. Alternatives are measured against the objectives to determine which possible solution is best, and identify the value and trade-offs that may exist between solutions.

Effectiveness Measures

Measures of effective problem solving include:

- confidence of the participants in the problem solving process,

- selected solutions meet the defined objectives and solve the root cause of the problem,

- new solution options can be evaluated effectively using the problem solving framework, and

- the problem solving process avoids making decisions based on unvalidated assumptions, preconceived notions, or other traps that may cause a sub-optimal solution to be selected.

Systems Thinking

Purpose

Understanding how the people, processes, and technology within an organization interact allows business analysts to understand the enterprise from a holistic point of view.

Definition

Systems theory and systems thinking suggest that a system as a whole has properties, behaviours, and characteristics that emerge from the interaction of the components of that system. These factors are not predictable from an understanding of the components alone. For example, just because a business analyst knows that a customer may return an item they purchased doesn't give the business analyst the full picture. The analyst must analyze the impact the return has on such items as inventory, finance, and store clerk training. In the context of systems theory, the term system includes the people involved, the interactions between them, the external forces affecting their behaviour, and all other relevant elements and factors.

Effectiveness Measures

Measures of effective use of systems thinking include:

- communicating how a change to a component affects the system as a whole,

- communicating how a change to a system affects the environment it is in, and

- communicating how systems adapt to internal and/or external pressures and changes.

Conceptual Thinking

Purpose

Business analysts routinely receive large amounts of detailed and potentially disparate information. They apply conceptual thinking skills to find ways to understand how that information fits into a larger picture and what details are important, and to connect seemingly abstract information.

Definition

Conceptual thinking is about understanding the linkage between contexts, solutions, needs, changes, stakeholders, and value abstractly and in the big picture. It involves understanding and connecting information and patterns that may not be obviously related. Conceptual thinking involves understanding where details fit into a larger context. It involves using past experiences, knowledge, creativity, intuition, and abstract thinking to generate alternatives, options, and ideas that are not easily defined or related.

Conceptual thinking in business analysis is specifically about linking factors not easily defined to the underlying problem or opportunity, models, or frameworks that help stakeholders understand and facilitate themselves and others through change. It is needed to connect disparate information from a multitude of stakeholders, objectives, risks, details, and other factors. With this information it generates options and alternatives for a solution, and communicates this information to others while encouraging them to generate ideas of their own.

Effectiveness Measures

Measures of effective conceptual thinking include:

- connecting disparate information and acting to better understand the relationship,

- confirming the confidence and understanding of the concept being communicated with stakeholders,

- formulating abstract concepts using a combination of information and uncertainty, and

- drawing on past experiences to understand the situation.

Visual Thinking

Purpose

The ability to communicate complex concepts and models into understandable visual representations allows business analysts to engage stakeholders and help them understand the concepts being presented.

Definition

Visual thinking skills allow business analysts to create graphical representations of the concepts or systems being discussed. The goal of these graphical representations is to allow stakeholders to easily understand the concepts being presented, and then provide input. Visual thinking requires that the analyst make abstractions and then find suitable graphic devices to represent them.

Visual thinking is visualizing and creating simple visual concepts, graphics, models, diagrams, and constructs to convey and integrate non-visual information. In performing business analysis, large amounts of information and complex connections between contexts, stakeholders, needs, solutions, changes, and value are communicated. Visuals represent this information and its complexities, allowing stakeholders and audiences to learn more quickly, process the information, and connect points from each of their contexts.

Visual thinking also allows the audience to engage and connect concepts more quickly and freely into their context, as well as understand and appreciate others' contexts more clearly.

Effectiveness Measures

Measures of effective visual thinking include:

- complex information is communicated in a visual model which is understandable by stakeholders,
- visuals allow for comparisons, pattern finding, and idea mapping with participants,
- productivity increases due to increased learning, quick memory, and follow through from effective visuals,
- stakeholders are engaged at a deeper level than with text alone, and
- stakeholders understand critical information which may have been missed if presented in textual content alone.

A.2　Behavioural Characteristics

Behavioural characteristics are not unique to business analysis but they have been found to increase personal effectiveness in the practice of business analysis. These characteristics exist at the core of every business analyst's skill set. Each of the behavioural characteristics described here can impact the outcome of the practitioner's efforts.

The core competencies of behavioural characteristics focus on the skills and behaviours that allow a business analyst to gain the trust and respect of stakeholders. Business analysts do this by consistently acting in an ethical manner, completing tasks on time and to expectations, efficiently delivering quality results, and demonstrating adaptability to changing needs and circumstances.

Behavioural Characteristics core competencies include:

- Ethics,
- Personal Accountability,
- Trustworthiness,
- Organization and Time Management, and
- Adaptability.

Ethics

Purpose

Behaving ethically and thinking of ethical impacts on others allows business analysts to earn the respect of the stakeholders. The ability to recognize when a proposed solution or requirement may present ethical difficulties to an organization or its stakeholders is an important consideration that business analysts can use to help reduce exposure to risk.

Definition

Ethics require an understanding and focus on fairness, consideration, and moral behaviour through business analysis activities and relationships. Ethical behaviour includes consideration of the impact that a proposed solution can have on all stakeholder groups and working to ensure that those groups are treated as fairly as possible. Fair treatment does not require that the outcome be beneficial to a particular stakeholder group, but it does require that the affected stakeholders understand the reasons for decisions. Awareness of ethical issues allows business analysts to identify when ethical dilemmas occur and recommend resolutions to these dilemmas.

Effectiveness Measures

Measures of effective ethical behaviour include:

- prompt identification and resolution of ethical dilemmas,
- feedback from stakeholders confirming they feel decisions and actions are transparent and fair,
- decisions made with consideration of the interests of all stakeholders,
- reasoning for decisions that is clearly articulated and understood,
- full and prompt disclosure of potential conflicts of interest, and
- honesty regarding one's abilities, the performance of one's work, and accepting responsibility for failures or errors.

Personal Accountability

Purpose

Personal accountability is important for a business analyst because it ensures business analysis tasks are completed on time and to the expectations of colleagues and stakeholders. It enables the business analyst to establish credibility by ensuring that business analysis efforts meet the needs of the business.

Description

Personal accountability includes effectively planning business analysis work to achieve targets and goals, and ensuring that value delivered is aligned with business needs. It involves chasing down all leads and loose ends to fully satisfy the stakeholder's needs. Following through on and fully completing business analysis tasks produces complete, accurate, and relevant solutions traceable to a need. Business analysts take responsibility for identifying and escalating risks and issues. They also ensure that decision makers have the appropriate information in order to assess impact.

Effectiveness Measures

Measures of effective personal accountability include:

- work effort is planned and easily articulated to others,
- work is completed as planned or re-planned with sufficient reasoning and lead time,
- status of both planned and unplanned work is known,
- stakeholders feel that work is organized,
- risks and issues are identified and appropriately acted on,
- completely traceable requirements are delivered on time, and stakeholder needs are met.

Trustworthiness

Purpose

Earning the trust of stakeholders helps business analysts elicit business analysis information around sensitive issues and enables them to help stakeholders have confidence that their recommendations will be evaluated properly and fairly.

Description

Trustworthiness is the perception that one is worthy of trust. A business analyst being considered trustworthy may offset the natural fear of change experienced by many stakeholders.

Several factors can contribute to being considered trustworthy:

- intentionally and consistently completing tasks and deliverables on time, within budget, and achieving expected results so that colleagues and stakeholders consider the business analyst's behaviour dependable and diligent,

- presenting a consistent attitude of confidence, so that colleagues and stakeholders consider the business analyst's demeanor as strong,

- acting in an honest and straightforward manner, addressing conflict and concerns immediately so that colleagues and stakeholders consider the business analyst's morals as being honest and transparent, and

- maintaining a consistent schedule over a long period of time so that colleagues and stakeholders consider the business analyst's availability predictable and reliable.

Effectiveness Measures

Measures of effective trustworthiness include:

- stakeholders involve the business analyst in discussions and decision making,

- stakeholders bring issues and concerns to the business analyst,

- stakeholders are willing to discuss difficult or controversial topics with the business analyst,

- stakeholders do not blame the business analyst when problems occur,

- stakeholders respect the business analyst's ideas and referrals, and

- stakeholders respond to the business analyst's referrals with positive feedback.

Organization and Time Management

Purpose

Organization and time management skills help business analysts perform tasks effectively and use work time efficiently.

Description

Organization and time management involves the ability to prioritize tasks, perform them efficiently, and manage time effectively. Business analysts are constantly acquiring and accumulating significant quantities of information, and this information must be organized and stored in an efficient manner so that it can be used and reused at a later date. Business analysts must also be able to differentiate important information that should be retained from less important information.

Effective time management requires the ability to prioritize tasks and deadlines.

Techniques of organization include establishing short- and long-term goals, action plans, prioritizing tasks, and utilizing a checklist. Techniques for effective time management include establishing time limits on non-critical tasks, focusing more time on high risk and priority tasks, setting aside focus time, and managing potential interruptions.

Effectiveness Measures

Measures of effective organization and time management include:

- the ability to produce deliverables in a timely manner,
- stakeholders feel that the business analyst focuses on the correct tasks at the right time,
- schedule of work effort and deadlines is managed and communicated to stakeholders,
- stakeholders feel their time in meetings and in reading communications is well spent,
- complete preparation for meetings, interviews, and requirements workshops,
- relevant business analysis information is captured, organized, and documented,
- adherence to the project schedule and the meeting of deadlines,
- provides accurate, thorough, and concise information in a logical manner which is understood by stakeholders, and
- maintains up-to-date information on the status of each work item and all outstanding work.

Adaptability

Purpose

Business analysts frequently work in rapidly changing environments and with a variety of stakeholders. They adjust their behavioural style and method of approach to increase their effectiveness when interacting with different stakeholders, organizations, and situations.

Definition

Adaptability is the ability to change techniques, style, methods, and approach. By demonstrating a willingness to interact with and complete tasks in a manner preferable to the stakeholders, business analysts can maximize the quality of service delivered and more efficiently help the organization achieve its goals and objectives. Having the curiosity to learn what others need and possessing the courage to try a different behaviour is adapting to situations and context.

Business analysts sometimes have to modify the way they interact with stakeholders, such as the way they conduct interviews or the way they facilitate workshops. Different stakeholders have different levels of comfort with techniques that are in the business analysis tool kit. Some stakeholders are more visual and respond better to information that is represented visually in models, diagrams, and pictures. Other stakeholders are more verbal and prefer textual descriptions. Being able to determine which techniques will work and which will not, and then adapt accordingly increases the likelihood of a successful interaction.

In the event that the goals and objectives of the organization change, business analysts respond by accepting the changes and adapting to a new mandate. Similarly, when circumstances arise or unanticipated problems occur, business analysts adapt by altering their plans and identifying options that can be used to deliver maximum value. The business analyst adapts when the business or stakeholder needs change, or when the context of the goal or the objective changes. When the need itself changes, the business analyst adapts by altering the plans and the approach in order to ensure that value is provided and delivered as part of the solution.

Effectiveness Measures

Measures of effective adaptability include:

- demonstrating the courage to act differently from others,

- adapting to changing conditions and environments,

- valuing and considering other points of view and approaches,

- demonstrating a positive attitude in the face of ambiguity and change,

- demonstrating a willingness to learn new methods, procedures, or techniques in order to accomplish goals and objectives,

- changing behaviour to perform effectively under changing or unclear conditions,

- acquiring and applying new information and skills to address new challenges,

- acceptance of having changes made to tasks, roles and project assignments as organizational realities change,

- altering interpersonal style to highly diverse individuals and groups in a range of situations, and

- evaluating what worked, what did not, and what could be done differently next time.

A.3   Business Knowledge

Business knowledge is required for the business analyst to perform effectively within their business, industry, organization, solution, and methodology. Business knowledge enables the business analyst to better understand the overarching concepts that govern the structure, benefits, and value of the situation as it relates to a change or a need.

Business Knowledge underlying competencies include:

- Business Acumen,
- Industry Knowledge,
- Organization Knowledge,
- Solution Knowledge, and
- Methodology Knowledge.

Business Acumen

Purpose

Business analysis requires an understanding of fundamental business principles and best practices in order to ensure they are considered as solutions are reviewed.

Description

Business acumen is the ability to understand business needs using experience and knowledge obtained from other situations. Organizations frequently share similar practices, such as legal and regulatory requirements, finance, logistics, sales, marketing, supply chain management, human resources, and technology. Business acumen is the ability to understand and apply the knowledge based on these commonalities within differing situations.

Understanding how other organizations have solved challenges may be useful when seeking possible solutions. Being aware of the experiences or challenges encountered in the past may assist a business analyst in determining which information may be applicable to the current situation. Factors that may cause differences in practices can include industry, location, size of organization, culture, and the maturity of the organization.

Effectiveness Measures

Measures of effective business acumen include:

- demonstrating the ability to recognize potential limitations and opportunities,
- demonstrating the ability to recognize when changes to a situation may require a change in the direction of an initiative or effort,
- understanding the risks involved and the ability to make decisions on managing risks,

- demonstrating the ability to recognize an opportunity to decrease expenses and increase profits, and

- understanding the options available to address emerging changes in the situation.

Industry Knowledge

Purpose

Industry knowledge provides the business analyst with an understanding of current practices and activities within an industry, and similar processes across industries.

Description

Industry knowledge is an understanding of:

- current trends,
- market forces,
- market drivers,
- key processes,
- services,
- products,
- definitions,
- customer segments,
- suppliers,
- practices,
- regulations, and
- other factors that impact or are impacted by the industry and related industries.

Industry knowledge is also an understanding of how a company is positioned within an industry, and its impacts and dependencies, in regards to the market and human resources.

When developing knowledge about a particular industry, competitor, or company the following set of questions can provide guidance:

- Who are the top leaders in the industry?

- Which organizations promote or regulate the industry?

- What are the benefits of being involved with these organizations?

- Who is creating publicity releases, participating in conventions, and delivering marketing materials?

- What are the comparisons of products and services?

- What are the satisfaction indicators/benchmarking projects that are applicable?

- What are the suppliers, practices, equipment and tools used by each company, and why do they use them?

- What are the potential impacts of weather, political unrest, or natural disasters?

- Who are the target customers and are they the same for the competition?

- What impacts the seasonal cycles for production, marketing, and sales? Does it impact staffing or require changes in processes?

Effectiveness Measures

Measures of effective industry knowledge include:

- being aware of activities within both the enterprise and the broader industry,

- having knowledge of major competitors and partners,

- the ability to identify key trends shaping the industry,

- being familiar with the largest customer segments,

- having knowledge of common products and product types,

- being knowledgeable of sources of information about the industry, including relevant trade organizations or journals,

- understanding of industry specific terms, standards, processes and methodologies, and

- understanding of the industry regulatory environment.

Organization Knowledge

Purpose

Organization knowledge provides an understanding of the management structure and business architecture of the enterprise.

Definition

Organization knowledge includes an understanding of how the enterprise generates profits, accomplishes its goals, its organizational structure, the relationships that exist between business units, and the persons who occupy key stakeholder positions. Organization knowledge also includes understanding the organization's formal and informal communication channels as well as an awareness of the internal politics that influence decision making.

Effectiveness Measures

Measures of effective organization knowledge include:

- the ability to act according to informal and formal communications and authority channels,

- understanding of terminology or jargon used in the organization,

- understanding of the products or services offered by the organization,

- the ability to identify subject matter experts (SMEs) in the organization, and

- the ability to navigate organizational relationships and politics.

Solution Knowledge

Purpose

Solution knowledge allows business analysts to leverage their understanding of existing departments, environments, or technology to efficiently identify the most effective means of implementing a change.

Definition

When the business analysis effort involves improving an existing solution, business analysts apply knowledge and experience from the previous work on the solution. Familiarity with the range of commercially available solutions or suppliers can assist with the identification of possible alternatives. The business analyst may leverage knowledge gained from prior experiences to expedite the discovery of potential changes through elicitation or in-depth analysis.

Effectiveness Measures

Measures of effective solution knowledge include:

- reduced time or cost to implement a required change,

- shortened time on requirements analysis and/or solution design,

- understanding when a larger change is, or is not, justified based on business benefit, and

- understanding how additional capabilities that are present, but not currently used, can be deployed to provide value.

Methodology Knowledge

Purpose

Understanding the methodologies used by the organization provides the business analyst with information regarding context, dependencies, opportunities, and constraints used when developing a business analysis approach.

Description

Methodologies determine the timing (big steps or small increments), the approach, the role of those involved, the accepted risk level, and other aspects of how a change is approached and managed. Organizations adopt or create their own methodologies to fit varying levels of culture, maturity, adaptability, risk, uncertainty, and governance.

Knowledge regarding a variety of methodologies allows the business analyst to quickly adapt to, and perform in, new environments.

Effectiveness Measures

Measures of effective methodology knowledge include:

- the ability to adapt to changes in methodologies,

- the willingness to use or learn a new methodology,

- the successful integration of business analysis tasks and techniques to support the current methodology,

- familiarity with the terms, tools, and techniques prescribed by a methodology, and

- the ability to play multiple roles within activities prescribed by a methodology.

A.4   Communication Skills

Communication is the act of a sender conveying information to a receiver in a method which delivers the meaning the sender intended. Active listening skills help to deepen understanding and trust between the sender and the receiver. Effective communication benefits all stakeholders.

Communication may be accomplished using a variety of delivery methods: verbal, non-verbal, physical, and written. Most communication methods deal with words, while some methods deal with movements and expressions. Words, gestures, and phrases may have different meanings to different individuals. Effective communication involves both the sender and receiver possessing the same understanding of the information being communicated. A shared glossary of terms and clear goals are effective tools to avoid misunderstandings and the resulting complications.

Effective communication includes adapting communication styles and techniques to the knowledge level and communication styles of recipients. Effective communicators understand how tone, body language, and context change the meaning of words. Gaining an understanding of the terms and concepts (prior to the exchange) can provide fruitful benefits.

Planning effective communication includes the sender reviewing the information that is known about the receiver. Differences between the sender and the receiver, such as native language, culture, motivations, priorities, communication, learning, and thinking styles may call for specific communication methods. Each piece of information must be carefully crafted and packaged to ensure it is clear and understood.

When planning to communicate information, the following considerations may be helpful:

- consider what the receiver knows or does not know,

- structure the information in a logical, comprehensible manner,

- determine how to best present the information to convey the intended meanings (for example, using visual aids, graphs, diagrams, or bullet points), and

- understand the expectations of the recipients.

Communication Skills core competencies include:

- Verbal Communication,

- Non-Verbal Communication,

- Written Communication, and

- Listening.

Verbal Communication

Purpose

Business analysts use verbal communication to convey ideas, concepts, facts, and opinions to a variety of stakeholders.

Description

Verbal communication uses spoken words to convey information from the sender to the receiver. Verbal communication skills are used to express business analysis information, ideas, concepts, facts, and opinions. It allows for the efficient transfer of information, including emotional and other non-verbal cues. It can be paired with both written and non-verbal communication.

Verbal communication deals specifically with the sender's choice of words and the tone of voice. When the receiver is able to see the sender, the sender's non-verbal communication impacts the meaning of the message being understood by the receiver. When the sender is able to see the receiver, the receiver is providing a response and both the sender and receiver are engaged in a dialogue, even though the receiver may not be speaking verbally. Monitoring the receiver's non-verbal communication allows the sender to consider adapting the message for the receiver.

Having an understanding of the tone of the communication and how it can positively or negatively influence the listener allows the business analyst to more effectively communicate verbally. Effective verbal communication skills include the ability to make one's meaning understood. The sender should partner verbal communication with active listening to ensure that information presented is being understood by the receiver.

Effectiveness Measures

Measures of effective verbal communication include:

- restating concepts to ensure all stakeholders clearly understand the same information,

- assisting conversations to reach productive conclusions,

- delivering effective presentations by designing and positioning content and objectives appropriately, and

- communicating an issue's important points in a calm and rational manner, and presenting solution options.

Non-Verbal Communication

Purpose

Non-verbal communication skills enable the effective sending and receiving of messages through—but not limited to—body movement, posture, facial expressions, gestures, and eye contact.

Definition

Communication is typically focused upon words that are written or spoken. Non-verbal communication, however, is believed to convey much more meaning than words alone. Moods, attitudes, and feelings impact body movement and facial expressions. Non-verbal communication begins immediately when one person is able to see another. The effective use of non-verbal communication skills can present a trustworthy, confident, and capable demeanor. Being aware of non-verbal communication provides the opportunity to be aware and address the feelings of others that are not expressed verbally.

Observing gestures or expressions cannot provide a complete understanding of the message being expressed by these non-verbal cues. These cues are indicators of the feelings and intent of the communicator. For example, when a stakeholder's non-verbal communication does not agree with their verbal message, the business analyst may want to explore the conversation further to uncover the source of this disagreement.

Effectiveness Measures

Measures of effective non-verbal communication include:

- being aware of body language in others, but not assuming a complete understanding through non-verbal communication,

- intentional awareness of personal non-verbal communication,

- improving trust and communication as a result of non-verbal communication, and

- effectively addressing and resolving situations when a stakeholder's non-verbal communication does not agree with their verbal message.

Written Communication

Purpose

Business analysts use written communication to to convey ideas, concepts, facts, and opinions to variety of stakeholders.

Definition

Written communication is the practice of using text, symbols, models (formal or informal), and sketches to convey and share information. An understanding of the audience is beneficial to effectively use written communication. Presenting information and ideas requires selecting the correct words so the audience will understand the intended meaning. Written communication has the added challenge of presenting information at a time or place that is remote from the time and place it was created.

Effective written communication requires a broad vocabulary, strong grasp of grammar and style, and an understanding of the terms which will be understood by the audience. Written communication has the potential to convey a great deal of information; however, conveying information effectively is a skill which must be developed.

Effectiveness Measures

Measures of effective written communication include:

- adjusting the style of writing for the needs of the audience,
- proper use of grammar and style,
- choosing words the audience will understand the intended meaning of, and
- ability of the reader to paraphrase and describe the content of the written communication.

Listening

Purpose

Effective listening allows the business analyst to accurately understand information that is communicated verbally.

Definition

Listening is the process of not just hearing words but understanding their meaning in context. By exhibiting effective listening skills, business analysts not only have a greater opportunity to accurately understand what is being communicated, but also to demonstrate that they think what the speaker is saying is important.

Active listening involves both listening and interpreting what the other person is trying to communicate beyond the words used in order to understand the essence of the message. Active listening includes summarizing and repeating what was stated in different terms in order to ensure that both the listener and the speaker have the same understanding.

Effectiveness Measures

Measures of effective listening include:

- giving the speaker undivided attention,

- acknowledging the speaker with verbal or non-verbal encouragement,

- providing feedback to the person or the group that is speaking to ensure there is an understanding, and

- using active listening skills by deferring judgment and responding appropriately.

A.5   Interaction Skills

Interaction skills are represented by the business analyst's ability to relate, cooperate, and communicate with different kinds of people including executives, sponsors, colleagues, team members, developers, vendors, learning and development professionals, end users, customers, and subject matter experts (SMEs).

Business analysts are uniquely positioned to facilitate stakeholder communication, provide leadership, encourage comprehension of solution value, and promote stakeholder support of the proposed changes.

Interaction Skills core competencies include:

- Facilitation,

- Leadership and Influencing,

- Teamwork,

- Negotiation and Conflict Resolution, and

- Teaching.

Facilitation

Purpose

Business analysts facilitate interactions between stakeholders in order to help them make a decision, solve a problem, exchange ideas and information, or reach an agreement regarding the priority and the nature of requirements. The business analyst may also facilitate interactions between stakeholders for the purposes of negotiation and conflict resolution (as discussed in Negotiation and Conflict Resolution).

Definition

Facilitation is the skill of moderating discussions within a group in order to enable all participants to effectively articulate their views on a topic under discussion, and to ensure that participants in the discussion are able to recognize and appreciate the differing points of view that are articulated.

Effectiveness Measures

Measures of effective facilitation include:

- making it clear to the participants that the facilitator is a third party to the process and not a decision maker nor the owner of the topic,

- encouraging participation from all attendees,

- remaining neutral and not taking sides, but at the same time being impartial and intervening when required in order to make suggestions and offer insights,

- establishing ground rules such as being open to suggestions, building on what is there, not dismissing ideas, and allowing others to speak and express themselves,

- ensuring that participants in a discussion correctly understand each other's positions,

- using meeting management skills and tools to keep discussions focused and organized,

- preventing discussions from being sidetracked onto irrelevant topics, and

- understanding and considering all parties' interests, motivations, and objectives.

Leadership and Influencing

Purpose

Business analysts use leadership and influencing skills when guiding stakeholders during the investigation of business analysis information and solution options. They build consensus and encourage stakeholder support and collaboration during change.

Definition

Leadership and influencing involves motivating people to act in ways that enable them to work together to achieve shared goals and objectives. Understanding the individual motives, needs, and capabilities of each stakeholder and how those can be effectively channeled assists business analysts in meeting the shared objectives of the organization. The business analyst's responsibility for defining, analyzing, and communicating business analysis information provides opportunities for leadership and influencing, whether or not there are people formally reporting to the business analyst.

Effectiveness Measures

Measures of effective leadership and influencing include:

- reduced resistance to necessary changes,

- articulation of a clear and inspiring vision of a desired future state,

- success in inspiring others to turn vision into action,

- influence on stakeholders to understand mutual interests,

- effective use of collaboration techniques to influence others,

- influence on stakeholders to consider broader objectives over personal motivations, and

- re-framing issues so alternate perspectives can be understood and accommodated to influence stakeholders towards shared goals.

Teamwork

Purpose

Teamwork skills allow business analysts to work productively with team members, stakeholders, and any other vested partners so that solutions can be effectively developed and implemented.

Definition

Business analysts often work as part of a team with other business analysts, project managers, stakeholders, and subject matter experts (SMEs). Relationships with people in those roles are a critical part of the success of any project or enterprise. It is important for the business analyst to understand how a team is formed and how it functions. Recognizing team dynamics and how they play a part as the team progresses through various stages of a project is also crucial. Knowing and adapting to how and when a team is progressing through a project's life cycle can lower the negative influences that impact a team.

Building and maintaining trust of teammates contributes to the integrity of the team as a whole and helps the team perform at its fullest capacity. When team members actively foster an environment for positive and trusting team dynamics, difficult decisions and challenges become less complicated.

Team conflict is common. If handled well, the resolution of conflict can benefit the team. Resolving conflict requires the team to focus on examining the positions, assumptions, observations, and expectations of all team members. Working through such problems can have the beneficial effect of strengthening the foundation of the analysis and the solution.

Effectiveness Measures

Measures of effective teamwork include:

- fostering a collaborative working environment,

- effectively resolving conflict,

- developing trust among team members,

- support among the team for shared high standards of achievement, and

- promoting a shared sense of ownership of the team goals.

Negotiation and Conflict Resolution

Purpose

Business analysts occasionally mediate negotiations between stakeholders in order to reach a common understanding or an agreement. During this process, business analysts help resolve conflicts and differences of opinion with the intent of maintaining and strengthening working relationships among stakeholders and team members.

Definition

Negotiation and conflict resolution involves mediating discussions between participants in order to help them recognize that there are differing views on the topic, resolve differences, and reach conclusions that have the agreement of all participants. Successful negotiation and conflict resolution includes identifying the underlying interests of the parties, distinguishing those interests from their stated positions, and helping the parties identify solutions that satisfy those underlying interests. The business analyst accomplishes this while ensuring that the outcome of the resolution aligns with the overall solution and the business needs.

Effectiveness Measures

Measures of effective negotiation and conflict resolution include:

- a planned approach to ensure that the negotiation takes into account the tone of voice, the conveyed attitude, the methods used, and the concern for the other side's feelings and needs,

- the ability to recognize that the needs of the parties are not always in opposition and that it is often possible to satisfy both parties without either side losing,

- an objective approach to ensure the problem is separated from the person so that the real issues are debated without damaging working relationships, and

- the ability to recognize that effective negotiation and conflict resolution are not always achieved in a single autonomous meeting, and that sometimes several meetings are required in order to achieve the stated goals.

Teaching

Purpose

Teaching skills help business analysts effectively communicate business analysis information, concepts, ideas, and issues. They also help ensure that information is understood and retained by stakeholders.

Definition

Teaching is the process of leading others to gain knowledge. Business analysts are responsible for confirming that the information communicated has been understood by stakeholders. Business analysts lead stakeholders to discover clarity in ambiguity by helping them learn about the contexts and value of the needs being investigated. This requires teaching skills in selecting the most appropriate visual, verbal, written, and kinesthetic teaching approaches according to the information or techniques being taught. The intent is to draw out stakeholder engagement and collaborative learning to gain clarity. Business analysts frequently elicit and learn new information, and then teach this information to stakeholders in a meaningful way.

Effectiveness Measures

Measures of effective teaching include:

- utilizing different methods to communicate information to be learned by stakeholders,

- discovering new information through high levels of stakeholder engagement,

- validating that audiences have a clear understanding of the key messages that are intended to be learned, and

- verifying that the stakeholders can demonstrate the new knowledge, facts, concepts, and ideas.

A.6   Tools and Technology

Business analysts use a variety of software applications to support communication and collaboration, create and maintain requirements artifacts, model concepts, track issues, and increase overall productivity.

Requirements documentation is often developed using word processing tools, while the process of developing business requirements may require the use of prototyping and simulation tools, as well as specialized tools for modelling and diagramming.

Requirements management technologies support requirements workflow, approvals, baselining, and change control. These technologies can also support the traceability between requirements and assist in determining the impact of changes to requirements.

Interacting with the stakeholders and team members may require the use of communication and collaboration tools, as well as presentation software in order to showcase ideas and generate discussion among stakeholders and team members.

Business Analysis Tools and Technology core competencies include:

- Office Productivity Tools and Technology,

- Business Analysis Tools and Technology, and

- Communication Tools and Technology.

Office Productivity Tools and Technology

Purpose

Business analysts use office productivity tools and technology to document and track information and artifacts.

Definition

Office productivity tools and technology provide business analysts with the ability to organize, dissect, manipulate, understand, and communicate information clearly. Utilizing these tools requires becoming familiar with available resources. Understanding one software program may provide insights into comparable abilities or operations in similar programs. Additionally, some programs are designed to provide additional tools to other programs or exchange information, such as e-mail or programs that can import/export files. Many organizations utilize these tools to study, store, and distribute information.

Office productivity tools and technology include the following:

- Word processing and presentation programs: provide the ability to present information in the form of a letter, newspaper, poster, research paper, slide presentation, or animations. Word processors are commonly used to develop and maintain requirements documents, allowing a great deal of control over their formatting and presentation. Standard requirements documentation templates are widely available for word processors. Most word processing tools have a limited capability to track changes and record comments, and are not designed for collaborative authoring; however, there are cloud solutions that provide collaborative functionality.

- Presentation software: serves in the creation of training materials or to present information to stimulate discussion among stakeholders. Some of these applications can be used in a very limited way to capture requirements or create a basic prototype.

- Spreadsheets: allow mathematical and logical manipulation. They are often used to maintain lists (such as atomic requirements, features, actions, issues, or defects). They are also used to capture and perform basic manipulation of numeric data. They can support decision analysis, and are very effective at summarizing complex scenarios. They support limited change tracking and can be shared among multiple users in the same way as a word processing document.

- Communication tools (e-mail and instant messaging programs): provide the means to communicate with stakeholders who are remotely located, who cannot respond to queries immediately, or who may need a longer-term record of a discussion. They are generally available to almost all stakeholders and are very easy to use. However, they are generally not effective for long-term storage or retention of information. Their primary use is to facilitate communication over time or distance.

- Collaboration and knowledge management tools: support the capturing of knowledge distributed throughout an organization and make it as widely available as possible. They allow documents to be accessible by an entire team, and facilitate collaboration. They also enable multiple users to work on a document simultaneously, and generally support comments and discussion about document content. These tools may take the form of a document repository (which integrates with office productivity software), wikis (which allow easy creation and linking of web pages), discussion forums, cloud services, or other web-based tools.

- Hardware: allows for the replication and distribution of information to facilitate communication with stakeholders. Tools such as printers and digital projectors are often used to translate digital information generated on a computer into physical information for ease of use. Photocopiers and scanners copy physical documents and can provide the ability to share them electronically.

Effectiveness Measures

Measures of effective office productivity tools and technology include:

- increased efficiencies and streamlining of processes by exploring features and functions of tools,

- awareness of available tools, their operation, and abilities,

- the ability to determine the tool that will best meet stakeholder needs, and

- the ability to clearly communicate the major features of available tools.

Business Analysis Tools and Technology

Purpose

Business analysts use a variety of tools and technology to model, document, and manage outputs of business analysis activities and deliverables to stakeholders.

Definition

Tools that are specific to the field of business analysis provide specialized capabilities in:

- modelling,

- diagramming,

- documenting,

- analyzing and mapping requirements,

- identifying relationships between requirements,

- tracking and storing requirements artifacts, and

- communicating with stakeholders.

Some business analysis tools and technologies focus solely on a single business analysis activity and some integrate multiple business analysis functions into a single tool. Tools specifically designed for business analysis may include such functionality as modelling, requirements management, issue tracking, prototyping and simulation, computer aided software engineering (CASE), and survey engines.

Modelling tools can provide functionality that assists business analysts with a number of modelling related tasks, including:

- creating models and visuals to help align stakeholders and outline the relationship of needs, entities, requirements, stakeholders, and context,

- tracing visuals to business rules, text requirements, scope statements, scope visuals, data requirements, product needs, and other requirements context and information, and

- creating an executable for a proprietary engine in order to execute the model or generate an application code which can be enhanced by a developer.

These tools frequently validate compliance with the notation. Some modelling tools support the creation of executable models, such as business process management systems (which allow for the creation of executable process models) and business rules management systems (which allow for the evaluation of captured business rules).

Requirements management technologies can provide functionality that assists business analysts with a number of requirements management related tasks including:

- requirements workflow including baselining, approvals and sign-off, change control, and implementation status,

- traceability including backwards traceability, forwards traceability, relationships between requirements, and impact analysis of requirements change,

- configuration management of requirements and requirements artifacts, and

- verifying the quality of requirements through checking for defined characteristics and relationships.

Issue tracking tools can provide functionality that assists business analysts with a number of issue tracking related tasks such as:

- tracking requirements risks,

- tracking requirements conflicts and issues, and

- tracking defects.

Prototyping and simulation tools can provide functionality that assists business analysts with prototyping or simulating the solution or pieces of the solution.

Effectiveness Measures

Measures of effective business analysis tools and technology include:

- the ability to apply an understanding of one tool and other similar tools,

- being able to identify major tools currently available and describe their strengths, weaknesses, and how they may be used in any given situation,

- understanding of and the ability to use the major features of the tool,

- ability to select a tool or tools that support organizational processes,

- the ability to use the tools to complete requirements-related activities more rapidly than otherwise possible, and

- the ability to track changes to the requirements and their impact on the solution implementation, stakeholders, and value.

Communication Tools and Technology

Purpose

Business analysts use communication tools and technology to perform business analysis activities, manage teams, and collaborate with stakeholders.

Definition

Communication tools are used to plan and complete tasks related to conversational interactions and collaborative interactions. Communication tools allow business analysts to work with virtual and co-located teams.

Understanding the options available with these tools—and knowing how to use various communications tools to complete tasks and utilize various techniques in a variety of collaboration environments—can enable more efficient and accurate communication and more effective decision making. Business analysts select the appropriate tool and technology for the situation and stakeholder group while balancing cost, risk, and value.

Examples of conversation interaction tools include voice communications, instant messaging, online chat, e-mail, blogging, and microblogging.

Examples of collaboration tools include video conferencing, electronic white boarding, wikis, electronic calendars, online brainstorming tools, electronic decision making, electronic voting, document sharing, and idea sharing.

Effectiveness Measures

Measures of effective communication tools and technology include:

- the selection of appropriate and effective tools for the audience and purpose,

- effectively choosing when to use communication technology and when not to,

- the ability to identify tools to meet communication needs, and

- understanding of and the ability to use features of the tool.

Appendix B: Glossary

b

behavioural characteristics: Your demonstrated character traits on the job that are observed by others or by you.

benchmarking: A comparison of a decision, process, service, or system's cost, time, quality, or other metrics to those of leading peers to identify opportunities for improvement.

brainstorming: A team activity that seeks to produce a broad or diverse set of options through the rapid and uncritical generation of ideas.

business analysis: The practice of enabling change in the context of an enterprise by defining needs and recommending solutions that deliver value to stakeholders.

business analysis effort: The scope of activities a business analyst is engaged in during the life cycle of an initiative.

business analysis information: Any kind of information at any level of detail that is used as an input to business analysis work, or as an output of business analysis work.

business analyst: Any person who performs business analysis, no matter their job title or organizational role.

business architecture: The design, structure, and behaviour of the current and future states of an enterprise to provide a common understanding of the organization. It is used to align the enterprise's strategic objectives and tactical demands.

business process: An end-to-end set of activities which collectively responds to an event, and transforms information, materials, and other resources into outputs that deliver value directly to the customers of the process. It may be internal to an organization, or it may span several organizations.

c

capability: The set of activities the enterprise performs, the knowledge it has, the products and services it provides, the functions it supports, and the methods it uses to make decisions.

change: The act of transformation in response to a need.

change control: Controlling changes to requirements and designs so that the impact of requested changes is understood and agreed-to before the changes are made.

checklist (business analysis): A standard set of quality elements that reviewers use for requirements verification.

collaboration: The act of two or more people working together towards a common goal.

common techniques: Method and procedures used to best demonstrate or perform the areas of expertise at the levels of proficiency.

component: A uniquely identifiable element of a larger whole that fulfills a clear function.

customer: A stakeholder who uses or may use products or services produced by the enterprise and may have contractual or moral rights that the enterprise is obliged to meet.

d

decision analysis: An approach to decision making that examines and models the possible consequences of different decisions, and assists in making an optimal decision under conditions of uncertainty.

design: A usable representation of a solution.

domain: The sphere of knowledge that defines a set of common requirements, terminology, and functionality for any program or initiative solving a problem.

e

elicitation: Iterative derivation and extraction of information from stakeholders or other sources.

enterprise: A system of one or more organizations and the solutions they use to pursue a shared set of common goals.

evaluation: The systematic and objective assessment of a solution to determine its status and efficacy in meeting objectives over time, and to identify ways to improve the solution to better meet objectives. See also indicator; metric, monitoring.

f

facilitation: The art of leading and encouraging people through systematic efforts toward agreed-upon objectives in a manner that enhances involvement, collaboration, productivity, and synergy.

i

impact analysis: An assessment of the effects a proposed change will have on a stakeholder or stakeholder group, project, or system.

initiative: A specific project, program, or action taken to solve some business problem(s) or achieve some specific change objective(s).

input (business analysis): Information consumed or transformed to produce an output. An input is the information necessary for a task to begin.

l

life cycle: A series of changes an item or object undergoes from inception to retirement

m

methodology: A body of methods, techniques, procedures, working concepts, and rules used to solve a problem

model: A representation and simplification of reality developed to convey information to a specific audience to support analysis, communication, and understanding.

monitoring: Collecting data on a continuous basis from a solution in order to determine how well a solution is implemented compared to expected results.

n

need: A problem or opportunity to be addressed.

o

organization: An autonomous group of people under the management of a single individual or board, that works towards common goals and objectives.

p

plan: A detailed scheme for doing or achieving something usually comprising a set of events, dependencies, expected sequence, schedule, results or outcomes, materials and resources needed, and how stakeholders need to be involved.

process: A set of activities designed to accomplish a specific objective by taking one or more defined inputs and turning them into defined outputs.

project: A temporary endeavour undertaken to create a unique product, service, or result.

prototype: A partial or simulated approximation of the solution for the purpose of eliciting or verifying requirements with stakeholders.

q

quality: The degree to which a set of inherent characteristics fulfills needs.

r

repository: A real or virtual facility where all information on a specific topic is stored and is available for retrieval.

requirement: A usable representation of a need.

requirements management: Planning, executing, monitoring, and controlling any or all of the work associated with requirements elicitation and collaboration, requirements analysis and design, and requirements life cycle management.

requirements traceability: The ability for tracking the relationships between sets of requirements and designs from the original stakeholder need to the actual implemented solution. Traceability supports change control by ensuring that the source of a requirement or design can be identified and other related requirements and designs potentially affected by a change are known.

requirements workshop: A structured meeting in which a carefully selected group of stakeholders collaborate to define and/or refine requirements under the guidance of a skilled neutral facilitator.

risk (business analysis): The effect of uncertainty on the value of a change, a solution, or the enterprise. See also residual risk.

root cause: The cause of a problem having no deeper cause, usually one of several possible causes.

s

scope: The boundaries of control, change, a solution, or a need.

service (business analysis): The performance of any duties or work for a stakeholder, from the perspective of the stakeholder.

solution: A specific way of satisfying one or more needs in a context.

stakeholder: A group or individual with a relationship to the change, the need, or the solution.

system: A set of interdependent components that interact in various ways to produce a set of desired outcomes.

t

technique: A manner, method, or style for conducting a business analysis task or for shaping its output.

traceability: See requirements traceability.

transition requirement: A requirement that describes the capabilities the solution must have and the conditions the solution must meet to facilitate transition from the current state to the future state, but which are not needed once the change is complete. They are differentiated from other requirements types because they are of a temporary nature.

V

validation (business analysis): The process of checking that a deliverable is suitable for its intended use. See also requirements validation.

value (business analysis): The worth, importance, or usefulness of something to a stakeholder in a context.

Appendix C: Contributors

The IIBA Competency Model Committee primarily developed content for this release. Members of the Committee who have generously volunteered their time and passion in the development of this release include:

SkillDirector

- Cheryl Lasse
- Stuart Rogers

Core Working Team

- Emily Iem, CBAP
- Diana Harvison, CBAP
- Tim Coventry, CBAP
- Jas Phul, CBAP
- Deb Oliver, CABP

Editors

- Vic Bhai

Practitioner Reviewers

- Barbara Monaco, CBAP
- Jennifer Battan, CBAP
- Tom Karasmanis
- Suzanna Rawlins, CBAP
- Zoya Roytblat, CBAP
- Tracy Watson, CBAP
- Rick Clare, CBAP
- Jennifer Colburn, CBAP
- Ted Hardy, MBA, CBAP
- Anthony Clarke, CBAP, PMI-PBA, CSTE, CSQA

Additional Thanks

IIBA® and the BA Competency Model Committee would like to thank all those practitioners of business analysis who have provided us with comments and feedback over the years, as well as those who have provided us with feedback on the public review draft.

Version 3.0

Version 3 Authors

- Kevin Brennan, CBAP, OCEB, PMP, Vice President, Professional Development
- Tim Coventry
- James R. Hughes
- Tom Karasmanis
- Angela M. Wick CBAP, PMP, Chair of Competency Model Committee

Version 3 Editor

- Ellie M. Bayrd

Version 3 Reviewers

- Nicole Batchelor
- Subroto Bose
- Roger T. Burlton, P.Eng, CMC
- Christopher Chan
- Rick Clare, OCP, PMP, CBAP
- Ingrid Colquitt, CBAP
- Jennifer C. Colburn, CBAP, PMP
- Ted Hardy, CBAP
- Tammis J. Lewis
- Michael Lindberg
- Tatiana Mezin
- Suzanna Rawlins, PMP, CBAP, CBPP
- Zoya Royblat, CBAP
- Julian Sammy
- Tracy Watson
- Maria Wintheiser

Version 2.0

Version 2 Authors

- Kevin Brennan, CBAP, OCEB, PMP, Vice President, Professional Development
- Jennifer C. Colburn, CBAP, PMP
- Tim Coventry
- James R. Hughes
- Joe Newbert
- Suzanna E. Rawlins, PMP, CBAP, CBPP
- Zoya Royblat, CBAP
- Angela M. Wick, CBAP, PMP, Chair of Competency Model Committee

Version 2 Reviewers

- Brian Lawrence
- Robert D'Alton
- Mario Santos
- Lisa Hankes
- Campbell Ferenbach, CBAP
- Miles Barker
- Russ Pena, CBAP
- Ingrid Colquitt, CBAP
- Subroto Bose
- Tatiana Mezin
- Tracy Watson
- Brendan Moon
- Anthony Migliardi
- Ted Hardy, CBAP
- Maria Wintheiser
- Michael Lindberg

Version 1.0

Version 1 Authors

- Kevin Brennan, CBAP, OCEB, PMP, Vice President, Professional Development
- Jennifer C. Colburn, CBAP, PMP

- James R. Hughes
- Tom Karasmanis
- Suzanna E. Rawlins, PMP, CBAP, CBPP
- Deborah Roberts
- Deborah L. Rose
- Thomas F. Ryder
- Julian Sammy
- Angela M. Wick, CBAP, PMP, Chair of Competency Model Committee

Version 1 Reviewers

- Kathleen Barret
- Tammy S. Bishop, CBAP
- Tim Coventry
- Vincent Kelly Cummins
- Ted Hardy, CBAP
- Michael Gladstone, CBAP
- Michael Lindberg
- Russ Pena, CBAP
- Maria Wintheiser
- Kelly Young, PMP